• Bartholomew

WALK THE WATERWAYS AROUND MANCHESTER

by David Perrott

Bartholomew

A Division of HarperCollins*Publishers*

CONTENTS

Fieldwork assistants: Jane & Jonathan Mosse

All walks devised by David Perrott

Illustrations by Morag Perrott

We wish to thank all the following for their help in checking these walks: Derek Cochrane & Veronica Lewis of British Waterways North West, and the relevant Canal Managers; Mike Webb of the Manchester Ship Canal Company; David Perry of the Rochdale Canal Company. The relevant departments of these borough, metropolitan or city councils: Ashton-under-Lyne; Bradford; Bury; Cheshire; Derbyshire; Lancashire; Oldham; Rochdale; Salford; Stockport; Trafford and Wigan. Also the Greater Manchester Countryside Unit.

A catalogue record for this book is available from the British Library.

Published by Bartholomew.
a Division of HarperCollins*Publishers*,
12 Duncan Street, Edinburgh, EH9 1TA.

First published 1992

© Bartholomew 1992

ISBN 0 7028 1809 7

Printed in Great Britain by Bartholomew,
HarperCollins*Manufacturing*, Edinburgh.

Produced for Bartholomew by
Perrott CartoGraphics, Darowen, Machynlleth SY20 8NS.

Typesetting: Perrott CartoGraphics and Litho Link
Litho origination: Litho Link, Leighton, Welshpool SY21 8HJ.

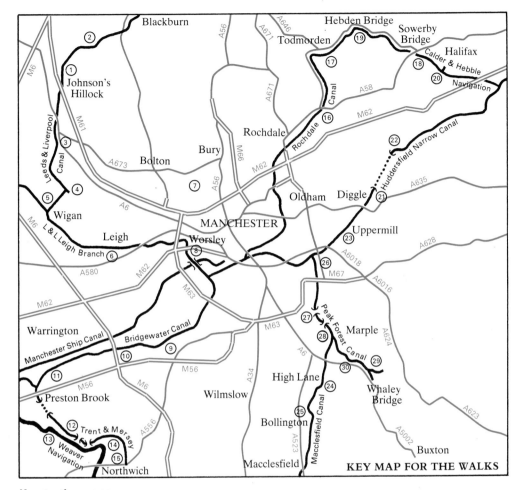

KEY MAP FOR THE WALKS

Key to the maps

All maps are drawn on a north axis, ie. with north at the top

Two scales are used — 1:25,000 and 1:31,680 — and are indicated on each route

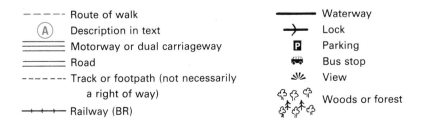

– – – –	Route of walk	▬▬▬▬	Waterway
(A)	Description in text	⤙	Lock
═══	Motorway or dual carriageway	P	Parking
═══	Road	🚌	Bus stop
– – – –	Track or footpath (not necessarily a right of way)	🌿	View
+–+–+–	Railway (BR)	🌳🌳🌳	Woods or forest

Walking the Waterways Around Manchester

The waterways of Manchester, built to supply the needs of the Industrial Revolution, now offer hard pressed city dwellers, and visitors, a quiet world of retreat and recreation. These ribbons of water, passing through towns, villages and open country, act as wildlife corridors, where plants and birds can exist relatively undisturbed. For the walker, towpaths, which once felt the steady plod of towing horses, now offer excellent level routes, sometimes high on embankments or deep in cuttings, through woods or open fields, or discreetly, often almost unnoticed, through the centre of a town or village.

There is interest for all - the moving patterns of light and reflections on the water itself, the natural history, the industrial archaeology, waterside pubs and, of course, the many different types of craft, from ocean going ships to traditional painted narrowboats.

For the inexperienced and experienced walker, whatever the season, these walks are packed with variety and interest. Virtually all the walks are circular, and every route contains a major component of waterside path – by canal, river, stream, lake or reservoir. You will visit pretty villages, country parks, quiet lanes, natural woodland and open moor. Tunnels, swing bridges, flights of locks and aqueducts are explored, and their history explained. There is even a stately home and a memorial to Lewis Carroll to see. Access is easy, the routes carefully planned, so why not walk them? You will not be disappointed.

1 WATERWAYS IN BRITAIN

The canal age in Britain began with the opening of the Bridgewater Canal in 1761. It was built by the Duke of Bridgewater to link his coal mines at Worsley with the burgeoning population of Manchester. Of course, river navigations, that is rivers deepened or widened to take boats, had been used since Roman times, but these followed natural routes which were often not convenient for the movement of goods, and were subject to spate or drought. Road transport was virtually non-existent, consisting of trains of pack horses making their way along poor unmade tracks. When the Bridgewater Canal opened, with its embankments and aqueducts constructed on a scale not seen since Roman times, it was a revelation. The price of coal in Manchester fell dramatically, fuelling the fires of the Industrial Revolution. The Duke's great investment paid off – the canal was a financial success, and suddenly everyone wanted to share in this transport revolution. You can visit this canal on Walks **8, 9, 10 & 11**.

The Trent & Mersey Canal, visited on Walks **12, 13, 14 & 15**, and the Staffordshire & Worcestershire Canal, both gained Royal Assent in 1766. The engineer James Brindley, who had designed the Bridgewater Canal, was employed as engineer for both of these canals and decided to build them to a narrow gauge. This decision, prompted both by the need for economy and well founded worries about water supplies, restricted the size of the locks (which dictate the maximum size of craft) to 72 feet 7 inches by 7 feet 6 inches (22 by 2.3 m) and, ironically, ensured that the canal system could not compete when the railways were built a century later. The specially designed craft which used the new canals, the narrowboat, could carry a 30 ton (30,480 kg) payload hauled by just one horse – remarkable in its day but hopelessly uneconomical in later years.

Building the Trent & Mersey Canal was a vast undertaking. Some 93 miles (150 km) long it included five tunnels (the first canal tunnels to be built on a cross country route), three of which can be visited on Walks **12 & 13**. In 1875 the Trent & Mersey was linked to the River Weaver (see Walks **12 & 13**) by the Anderton Lift (see Walk **14**), one of the 'seven wonders' of the waterways.

The canals were built entirely by hand – dug out by gangs of itinerant workers called navigators, or 'navvies' as we now know them, who lived roughly but were highly paid. They spent a great deal of their time and money in the local taverns, their raucous behaviour often striking terror into quiet country people.

By 1790 canal mania gripped the country – many schemes which received the Royal Assent were never built, others which were built were poorly planned and badly engineered. Shortage of water was a constant problem, and supplies were jealously guarded using 'stop locks' such as that on Walk **13**. Cut-throat competition resulted in toll cutting battles. Many canals never made a penny profit, and were abandoned, or were later drained and converted into railway lines.

The great engineers, Telford, Rennie and Jessop, planned routes and built magnificent structures. Three canals crossed the Pennines. The first to be started (but the last to be finished) was the Leeds & Liverpool Canal. At 127 miles (204 km) long it was the longest canal ever built in this country by one company. Many of its interesting features can be seen on Walks **1**, **2**, **3**, **4**, **5** & **6**.

The first through route across the Pennines was provided by the Rochdale Canal, in 1804. This waterway crammed 92 locks into 33 miles (53 km), and can be visited on Walks **16**, **17** & **19**. In 1811 the Huddersfield Narrow Canal was completed, its opening delayed by the mighty struggle to build the Standedge Tunnel – at 5698 yards (5210 m) in length and 645 feet (197 m) above sea level this is the longest and highest canal tunnel in the world, visited on Walk **22**. Walks **21** & **23** also include stretches of this remarkable waterway route.

The Rochdale Canal joined the Calder & Hebble Canal at Sowerby Bridge, where some very handsome canal warehouses have been restored. You can see these on Walk **18**, and the attractive flight of three locks at Salterhebble nearby on Walk **20**.

The Peak Forest Canal was opened in 1800 to provide an outlet for the great limestone quarries at Doveholes. These quarries, 1000 feet (305 m) above sea level, were joined to the canal at Buxworth. The canal basins at Buxworth, currently being restored, are a remarkable survival, where it is easy to imagine narrowboats loading in the intricate docks, while their crews refreshed themselves in the nearby pub. Buxworth Basins are visited on Walk **29**, along with the terminus at Whaley Bridge. Walk **30** can be linked with Walk **29** to explore The Goyt Valley. On Walk **27** there is a rare opportunity to walk through a canal tunnel. The Peak Forest Canal joins the Ashton Canal near Portland Basin and here, on Walk **26**, you can see where the Huddersfield Narrow Canal starts its climb across the Pennines.

Considered to be one of Britain's greatest civil engineers, Thomas Telford planned the Macclesfield Canal, which is visited on Walks **24** & **25**. It was actually engineered by William Crosley, but bears all of Telford's hallmarks – a direct course of cuttings and embankments known as 'cut and fill' – with the locks grouped in one flight. It joins the Peak Forest Canal at Marple Junction, and this, together with the superb Marple flight of locks, is explored on Walk **28**.

With the 19th century came the rise of the railways and the decline of the canal system. Price cutting and engineering improvements by the canal companies were to no avail, and gradually the first closures began – canals disappearing altogether or being left as isolated and truncated strips of water such as the Manchester, Bolton & Bury Canal, explored on Walk **7**. The last great canal enterprise, the Manchester Ship Canal, was completed in 1894, allowing ocean going ships into the heart of the city. You will have a close up look at this on Walk **8**. Effective commercial carrying ended in the early 1960's, although a few small companies and individuals still trade. The great docks and wharfs of Manchester are being converted for other use.

Today it is the amenity value of the waterways that has brought about the retention of the network. British Waterways, local councils, the Inland Waterways Association, canal societies and local groups effectively campaign for improvement and restoration. Canals that have lain disused for many years, such as the Huddersfield Narrow and the Rochdale, and which were seen as an eyesore and a danger, are now being restored to navigation.

A handsome legacy of the latter days of

commercial carrying on the narrow canals, when whole families used to live on board, are the gaily painted narrowboats, decorated with their traditional motifs of roses and castles. Enthusiasts still maintain some original craft, and those lucky enough to see and hear a boat and butty (a motor boat towing an unpowered 'butty') underway will be diving for their cameras. The bright colours, ornate lettering, boldly printed tarpaulins and intricate ropework are a fine sight, and the distinctive 'thunk-thunk-thunk' sound of a single cylinder Bolinder diesel engine cannot fail to attract attention. Many modern boats keep the tradition of colour and style alive, making any collection of craft, at a junction or by an old and cosy canal pub, a heart-warming sight.

2 NATURAL HISTORY

The natural history interest of any area is always enhanced by the presence of water. Canal and river banks have their own special species, and the water itself provides a habitat for many plants, animals, insects and, of course, fish. The number of species of fish is largely controlled by the purity of the water, and the appearance of large numbers of anglers in the Manchester area each weekend during the season indicates that the water is generally clean. The common species such as roach, bream, dace and perch are found throughout the system – of an evening you may see rings of ripples as they rise to take insects and flies which have landed on the surface.

Water skaters, skimming over the surface, and water boatmen, swimming up-side-down just under the surface, are sure to be seen in summer in a quiet spot. Living entirely in the water, but breathing air, are the water spiders. They store air as a bubble enclosed by a web, which is brought down from the surface trapped between the legs and abdomen. Many flying insects hatch out and live initially in the water. Particularly interesting amongst these is the caddis fly, whose larvae live in little tubes of stone, grit and leaves which they cement together.

Dragonflies, who make their noisy flights over water on hot summer days, also begin life in the water, the larvae being voracious feeders.

There are not many native aquatic mammals but two of them, water voles and water shrews, may be seen in the quieter parts.

Many colourful wild flowers grow in or near the water. Great clumps of pond sedge up to four feet high appear in the spring, bursting with dark brown flower spikes. These are followed, in May, by the gaudy yellow flowers of the flag iris, growing in marshy, waterside places. A plant with similar leaves, but with much less eye-catching green flower spikes, is the sweet flag. Its leaves have a sweet smell when crushed – in medieval times it was spread over floors to mask less desirable odours.

Marsh marigolds and the shiny yellow lesser celandine grow in shady spots but sparkle when caught by the sun. Other colours are introduced by the shaggy purple loosestrife; comfrey, with its dangling bell shaped flowers of white, pink and purple; the blue greater skullcap; the mauve marsh woundwort; white gypsywort; yellow bur marigold; greenish-white angelica and mauve water mint. *None* of these should be picked – enjoy them in situ and leave them to grow and propagate.

Water lilies are rooted in the bed of the canal, river or lake, their circular floating leaves providing a canopy under which fish love to hide. The yellow water lily is the most common – the shape of its seed capsules giving it the nickname 'brandy bottle'. Growing entirely under the water is the hornwort, with finely divided leaves and tiny flowers. Similar, although its tiny spikes of flowers poke out just above the surface, is the water milfoil.

At some stage, as you proceed along the water's edge, you are sure to disturb a heron, a large grey and white bird which will rise from the shallows with slow, noisy flaps of the wings. Other characteristic sights are the ripples left by a diving dab chick, the white tail of a moorhen disappearing into the reeds or, if you are *very* lucky, the vivid flash of sapphire as a kingfisher skims over the water. This, considered by many to be the most handsome of British birds, is a very shy creature, and your glimpse will not usually allow you to enjoy a close examination of its brick red underside, bright red feet and flash of white behind the eye. They catch fish in a shallow dive, beating their prey to death on a branch and swallowing it head first, to avoid choking on the fins and scales. When the water has been frozen for long periods, many kingfishers have been known to starve to death. They nest during the summer in holes in the river or canal bank.

Amongst the ducks, swans and geese, the ubiquitous mallard is well worth a mention. Although the females are a dull mottled brown, their mates are brightly coloured and handsome, with a bottle green head, white collar and grey body. They fraternise happily with white Aylesburys and both will be delighted to finish off the remnants of your sandwiches.

Finally, if your friends are not keen birdwatchers, you may wish to impress them by being able to tell the difference between moorhens and coots, two species which are, superficially, very similar. Coots are slightly the larger of the two, and are entirely black except for a white bill. The moorhen has a brownish back, a white line along its side and white under its tail, and a red and yellow beak. Its name derives from mere hen, the lake bird.

3 PATHS IN THE SOUTH PENNINES

The vast range of paths and tracks in the southern Pennines have their origins in pre-industrial revolution times. The production of cloth, now centred at sources of cheap power and transport, and with ready access to raw materials and markets, was once confined to individual and often remote homesteads. Here a family produced, on a single handloom, as little as one piece of cloth a week which had to be sold in order to finance the following week's housekeeping. This hand to mouth existence made good internal communications essential, and a series of all-weather paths grew up linking outlying dwellings, villages, farms, the church and often the pub. The abundance of local stone led to some of these paths becoming paved, often in quite remote and desolate areas, and they have become known as 'causey's', from the same root as the word causeway. The difficult terrain was not suited to the use of wheeled vehicles, so the pack horse became the primary means of transport following similar paved routes. Both have their origins in the 15th and 16th centuries. Later, with the coming of the industrial revolution, the wife and children within a particular family relied upon these paths on their journey to work in the neighbouring mill, leaving the husband at home still producing cloth on the handloom.

This fundamental need for dependable, well surfaced paths, dating back over many centuries, has led to the range and variety of routes that today offer the walker such a richness and diversity of choice.

4 THE COUNTRY CODE

Enjoy the countryside and respect its life and work.
Guard against all risk of fire.
Leave gates as you find them.
Keep your dogs under proper control.
Keep to public paths across farmland.
Use gates and stiles to cross fences, hedges and walls.
Leave livestock, crops and machinery alone.
Take your litter home.
Help to keep all water clean.
Protect wildlife, plants and trees.
Take special care on country roads.
Make no unnecessary noise.

5 SAFETY AND EQUIPMENT

You can enjoy the walks in this book without having to make an expensive investment in lots of clothing and equipment. All of these routes can be completed during the summer in sensible ordinary shoes, training shoes or wellington boots. During the winter (or a rainy spell of summer weather), however, many paths become muddy, especially so when they are close to canals, rivers or lakes. Since all of these walks include such paths, a good pair of walking boots is advisable.

The Manchester area receives a fair amount of rain, so do take a good waterproof anorak with you. Waterproof overtrousers can also contribute greatly to your comfort. Gloves and a warm hat, and spare clothing are recommended for winter walking.

A light weight rucksack is the best way to carry the things you need on a walk, leaving your hands free for negotiating gates and stiles. A small one will do for these walks. Use it to carry something to drink, high energy food such as chocolate, fruit and nut bars, or just your sandwiches. A simple first aid kit of patches and antiseptic cream is also a good idea – in summer thorns and brambles often overhang paths, and can scratch the unwary!

Note that where approximate distances are given in walk directions, the metric equivalents are also approximate: eg. 100 yards or 90 metres.

Walking beside water is a great pleasure – it is relaxing and always interesting, but *young children must be closely supervised at all times*, especially near locks, where the water is deep, the stonework slippery when wet, and there is sometimes exposed machinery.

Dog owners are also reminded that if they allow their animal to bound around unsupervised, it can cause accidents. Please keep your dog on a lead *at all times* near the water.

land. If you have a dog, ensure that it does not foul the footpath, and keep it on a lead, especially near water, where dogs can frighten children and cause them to step backwards without thinking. The Animals Act (1971) states that dogs considered to be a danger to livestock may be shot. The Protection of Livestock Act (1953) makes it an offence to permit a dog to worry livestock, with a maximum fine of £200.

British Waterways control the majority of waterways visited on these walks. It is their policy to encourage and optimise their use in as many ways and by as many people as possible. Where they exist, towpaths are regarded as being integral to the waterways and subject to British Waterways general duties and powers, and will be maintained as such for public recreational use by walkers, anglers, cyclists and others who desire access. Some towpaths are public footpaths or bridleways and will always retain that status. The others which have not been dedicated as public rights of way have been used for many years on a permissive basis, and this will continue.

Access to the countryside is becoming more and more vital as a means of relaxation in a hectic society. The great majority of footpaths in the area covered by this book are well maintained and signposted. If you do come across an obstruction, however, please report it to either the local highway authority, which is the respective County Council, or to the **Ramblers' Association**, 1-5 Wandsworth Road, London SW8 2XX, tel: 071 582 6878, who will deal with it. Most people don't like to follow obstructed paths, so these can become neglected and targets for extinguishment.

6 RIGHTS OF WAY

All the routes in this guide follow rights of way, well established concessionary paths, or towpaths. Always keep to the path and regard it as a privilege, as well as a right, to follow it across someone else's

7 TRANSPORT

Car parking information is given for each walk – if, at the time of going to press, a charge is made, this is mentioned. All the walks in this guide can be reached by public transport, and information regarding bus and train services is given in route instruction **1** of each walk. Bus services are especially liable to change, and it is essential that you check times and services *before setting out*. The relevant telephone number is given as appropriate. Enquire at your local BR station for train times and services.

Roads around Manchester are often heavily congested, and traffic jams occur frequently. The area has an excellent system of public transport, and using it is the rambler's way of safeguarding the countryside from having yet more roads built, and from damaging pollution. It is also important to support public transport since, for some, it is the only means of access to the countryside.

Enquire about bargain tickets, such as the 'Sunday Adventurer' from Cheshire Bus, or Rail Rovers from British Rail, which offer remarkably good value. Again, use the telephone numbers supplied, or ask at your local BR station.

8 USEFUL ADDRESSES

The relevant Weathercall telephone forecast can be obtained on 0898 500416 (charge).

Tourist information is available from:
Blackburn King George's Hall, Northgate, Blackburn, Lancashire BB2 1AA. Tel: 0254 53277.
Halifax Piece Hall, Halifax, W Yorkshire HX1 1RE. Tel: 0422 368725.
Hebden Bridge 1 Bridge Gate, Hebden Bridge, W Yorkshire HX7 8EX. Tel: 0422 843831.

Macclesfield Town Hall, Market Place, Macclesfield, Cheshire SK10 1HR. Tel: 0625 500500.
Manchester Town Hall Extension, Lloyd Street, Manchester M60 2LA. Tel: 061-234 3157.
Runcorn 57-61 Church Street, Runcorn, Cheshire WA7 1LG. Tel: 0928 576776.
Todmorden 15 Burnley Road, Todmorden, Lancashire OL14 7BU. Tel: 0706 818181.
Warrington 21 Rylands Street, Warrington, Cheshire WA1 1EJ. Tel: 0925 36501.
Wigan Trencherfield Mill, Wigan Pier, Wigan, Lancashire WN3 4EL. Tel: 0942 825677.
They all provide information on accommodation, events, attractions and entertainments.

The navigation authority for the majority of waterways visited on these walks is:
British Waterways North West Region, Navigation Road, Northwich, Cheshire CW8 1BH. Tel: 0606 74321.
The Bridgewater Canal is administered by:
The Manchester Ship Canal Company Key West, Trafford Wharf Road, Manchester M17 1HH. Tel: 061-872 2411.
The Rochdale Canal is administered by:
The Rochdale Canal Company 75 Dale Street, Manchester M1 2HG. Tel: 061-236 2456.

The Inland Waterways Association campaigns for the restoration, retention and development of inland waterways in the British Isles, and their fullest commercial and recreational use.
IWA 114 Regent's Park Road, London NW1 8UQ. Tel: 071-586 2510/2556.

Walk 1

JOHNSON'S HILL LOCKS & WITHNELL FOLD

6 miles (9.7 km) Moderate

0   1 mile

0   1 km

Two charming villages linked by a rural, tree lined stretch of the Leeds & Liverpool Canal combine to make this a walk of particular charm and variety. The flight of seven locks at Johnson's Hill are possibly the most attractively arranged on the entire canal, whilst Withnell Fold provides a delightful setting for a group of estate built cottages, arranged around three sides of a spacious square. On the fourth side stands an old set of wooden stocks.

6 Go ahead through a gate and follow the track across a field and through another gate. Ignore the driveway forking left and go ahead down a hill and through a farm-yard to join the main road. Turn right and walk back into Higher Wheelton village and the Withy Trees pub on your left.

5 Cross the bridge and go uphill following the cobbled road, bending right then left. Notice the square bordered by pretty stone mill workers' cottages together with the stocks on your left. Continue uphill and where the cobbled road bears left turn right along an unmetalled lane.

4 Walk approximately 2.5 miles (4 km), along the well maintained towpath as the canal winds through tree lined banks until you reach bridge 88 beside a large stone mill.

3 Follow the towpath to a canal junction and cross over the derelict arm on the metal foot-bridge to rejoin the towpath with the Leeds & Liverpool Canal still on your right. Continue up the lock flight.

1 Start from the Withy Trees pub in Higher Wheelton, which lies midway between Blackburn and Chorley on the A674. Bus numbers 123 and 124 stop close by (for bus information ring 0772 263333).
With your back to the pub turn left and walk about 400 yards (370 m) to fork right down Whins Lane. Where the lane ends go straight ahead along a footpath into Wheelton village. Turn right beside a clock tower along Kenyon Lane to meet the canal on your right.

2 Go ahead to cross a road beside the Top Lock pub and join a path beside the canal. Climb a stile, follow the canal and after passing two locks join a metalled road. Turn left uphill then right down Dark Lane to rejoin the canal at bridge 80. Cross the bridge and turn right onto the towpath.

Leeds & Liverpool Canal

Withnell Fold

Higher Wheelton

A674

Top Lock Bridge

Johnson's Hillock

Over

Walk 1
JOHNSON'S HILL LOCKS & WITHNELL FOLD
Continued

Withnell Fold, on the Leeds & Liverpool Canal

A The Leeds & Liverpool Canal at this point has climbed more than 350 feet (105 m) above sea level from its beginnings in Liverpool Docks; the greater part of this ascent being through the 21 locks of the Wigan Flight (see Walk **4**).

From the top of these locks to the branch above bridge 80, the Leeds & Liverpool and Lancaster Canals combined along a common course in order to save money. It was originally intended that the Lancaster Canal should run from Kendal, in Cumbria, to Westhoughton, a few miles east of Wigan. However, a reluctance to construct a very costly aqueduct to carry the canal over the River Ribble at Preston meant that the northern and southern sections were never linked. Whilst the line

of the Leeds & Liverpool Canal continues up Johnson's Hill Locks, the old Lancaster Canal forks left.

The canal continues on its way to Leeds by way of Blackburn, Burnley, Skipton and Bingley, reaching a maximum height of 487 feet (148 m) above sea level on its climb over the Pennines. Its length of 127 miles (204 km) makes it easily the longest waterway ever constructed by a single company.

B Withnell Fold Nature Reserve has been developed from a series of filter beds and sludge lagoons constructed for the Wiggins Teape paper mills that used to operate on the other bank of the canal. Nature, together with some help from Lancashire County Council, has now reclaimed the area and an

imaginative series of trails and walkways has been laid out.

C Paper making has long been an important industry in the Roddlesworth Valley, and Withnell Paper Mill, established on the canal bank in 1840 at a place known as 'Engine Bottoms', was the forerunner of several large producers. Its main output was of wrapping grades and similar types of paper using rags for its principal raw material. Withnell Fold was constructed to provide housing for the paper mill workers and stands today as a delightful example of just how attractive a small industrial community can be: a model village on a most approachable scale, neat and well cared for.

Walk 2
CHERRY TREE
4 miles (6.4km) Easy

The industrial outskirts of Blackburn are soon left behind as a gentle climb takes you out into open countryside. Here you will enjoy fine views of the valley with its handsome mills. The return journey follows a pretty, wooded stretch of the Leeds & Liverpool Canal.

Map labels: Station, P (car park), A674, Cherry Tree, Leeds & Liverpool Canal, A6062, Feniscowles, (B), (A), Higher Broadhalgh, Broken Stone Road

4 Go ahead, following a line of pylons, and climb a gate. Turn right down a field to go through a gate to a bridge. Cross the canal and join the towpath to walk with the canal on your right. Continue on the towpath for almost 2 miles (3.2km). Leave at the third bridge, turning left to return to the station.

1 Start at Cherry Tree BR station, which is on the Colne to Preston line, 2 miles (3.2 km) south-west of Blackburn on the A 674. There is a car park at the station, and regular buses from Blackburn (for bus information ring 0722 263333).
Turn right out of the station to cross a canal bridge. Walk along the front of the works to join a track. Continue along the end of the school pitch and up a path behind some houses to join a road. Turn right, cross the road and after 100 yards (90m) turn left between two houses to follow a track uphill. Go over a stile, then go ahead to cross two more to meet the road.

2 Cross the road carefully and go straight ahead to the left of a farm. Cross a stone stile in the wall. Turn right and follow a hedge on your right. Look for another stone stile. Climb over and turn right down a track to a road. Follow this for 50 yards (45m) to a cottage. Turn left, hard back in the direction that you have come, to take a track round the FRONT of the house.

3 Take a path to cross a stile. Follow a wire fence on your left until it turns right over a disused railway, where you climb a stile. With your back to the stile aim diagonally left to some trees above the canal. Continue along the trees with the canal on your right. Look for a gap in a fence and descend to the canal bank. Where the canal bears right take a path to your left up through the trees to climb a stile.

B The two mills at Feniscowles were founded in 1865 and 1875. Coal and rags were delivered by a tram road linking the mills to the canal. The first to be built, the Sun Paper Mill, now manufactures flutings for corrugated cases and packaging from recycled paper. Its neighbour, the Star Mill, has progressed from newsprint to coated paper.

A The Roddlesworth Valley has been the site of paper mills since the middle of the 19th century. Paper-making grew up alongside the textile industry, making use of waste rags in the manufacturing process. The industry was far from popular, with the boiling of old ropes, rags, clay, straw and chemicals in the manufacturing process producing a filthy effluent which did little to help the plant and fish populations in the area.

Walk 3
ADLINGTON
5 miles (8 km) Moderate

0   1 mile
0   1 km

A pretty walk along a wooded stretch of canal is followed by a gentle climb towards the Pennine foothills, giving views over the valley of the River Yarrow. The return to Adlington, via woods and streams, adds contrast and variety.

2 Cross the canal and a railway. Turn right to follow a road towards a farmhouse. Notice a ladder stile on your right. Cross this and veer right to follow a hedge on your left. Look out for a stile on your left and cross this onto the golf course. *LOOK OUT FOR FLYING GOLF BALLS.* With your back to the stile, aim to the right of the stone club house.

3 Turn right down the drive. Where it bends right, go ahead along a track. Cross the second stile on your left just before three gates. Follow a wall to a gate. Cross a stile and turn right onto a track. Continue to a white house and bear left to follow a hedge to a stile (ignoring a path beside the house). Go through a gate at the next farm and turn left past the stables. Leave by a gate and go up a track to a road. Turn left and continue to the Bay Horse pub.

4 Go ahead to cross a motorway bridge. Bear right and continue to a lodge on your left. Take a track opposite. Go on to cross a stile and walk through some woods. Cross a stile and a motorway bridge. Descend through the woods to a kissing-gate. Go through a gate onto an unmetalled road and follow this down to a road.

5 Turn right and continue to a public footpath sign on your left beyond a row of cottages. Turn left downhill, over a stile and down a field to go through a gate. Follow a stream under a railway viaduct. Bear right to follow a wall on your left to a works gate. Bear right up to the road. Turn right and retrace your steps to the station.

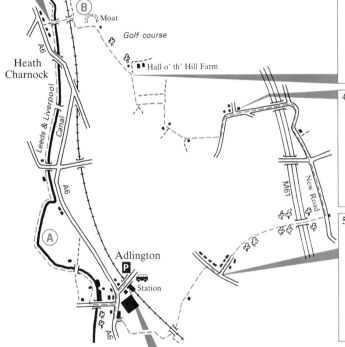

Heath Charnock

Leeds & Liverpool Canal

A6

Moat

Golf course

Hall o' th' Hill Farm

Adlington

Station

M61

New Road

A6

1 Start from Adlington BR station, which is on the Manchester to Preston line. The village lies on the A6 about 15 miles (24km) north-west of Manchester. Regular buses run here from Bolton (for bus information ring 0722 263333) and you may park in nearby streets.

Leave the station and turn left down to a junction. Turn left then right down Park Road. Cross a canal bridge and join the towpath to walk with the canal on your right. Continue under four bridges, then leave by some steps at the next bridge.

A This lock-free stretch of the Leeds & Liverpool Canal used to share its course with the Lancaster Canal, and became known as the Lancaster Pool.

B Notice the evidence of a moat around this old farm settlement.

Walk 4
THE WIGAN FLIGHT
6 miles (9.7km) Moderate

An industrial canal landscape is soon left behind as you are led across open farmland to a wooded hill, where the climb to the top offers superb panoramic views over rolling countryside. On your return the majestic woodland of Borsdane Nature Reserve makes a delightful culmination to this walk. This route can be linked with Walk 5 by walking down the flight of locks.

3 *Follow a path to your right to continue around the bottom of the hill but make a short diversion up the steps to enjoy the splendid view. Then return to the path. Continue through the woodland. Where the path leaves the wood fork left and look immediately for a stile in a fence on your left. Cross it. Go down the field with a fence on your left. Turn left over a stile and aim straight ahead into a hollow. Go through a stile next to a gate and continue uphill to another gate. Climb a stile and aim for a chapel ahead on the horizon. Turn right keeping a hedge on your left. Go through a stile to join a road.*

2 *Turn left down Farm Lane through a works yard. Bear left past a farm on your right to join the canal. Turn left and follow the towpath to Kirkless Hall pub. Turn right over the next bridge (no 58). Continue ahead to cross another canal bridge. Turn left after 50 yards (45 m) to follow a track between two wire fences. Go ahead along the boundary of a field. Where a fence on your left ends, turn right towards the end of a wooded hill.*

A The five locks on this short stretch of the Leeds & Liverpool Canal are the last of a long flight of 21, which raise the canal over 200 feet (60m). At the top of the flight the canal turns left to continue to Leeds. A short arm to the right is all that is left of a detached southern section of the Lancaster Canal.

4 *Cross the road and follow a public footpath around the end of a reservoir. Then keep straight ahead to some bungalows. Continue along the edge of the estate to take a path behind Dodd's Farm. Go ahead to some works and turn right at the gate on an unmetalled road.*

1 *Start from Hindley BR station, which is linked with Manchester and Wigan. Parking is available in the streets nearby. The no 38 bus from Manchester stops here (Mon - Sat daytime only, for information ring Busline, 061-228 7811).*
From the station turn right up a hill. Turn left at the golf club and go straight ahead. Fork right and follow a hedge along the side of the golf course. Bear right where the path forks and left along a row of cottages. Ignore a public footpath to the left but fork left in front of a new house towards the works. Follow a road to cross a canal bridge.

5 *Fork right into Borsdane Wood Nature Reserve. Follow the wide, well used path through the wood alongside a stream for 1.5 miles (2.4 km). Pass under a railway viaduct and turn immediately right at the end of a brick wall. Go up some steps and follow a path, climbing alongside an embankment, to return to the station.*

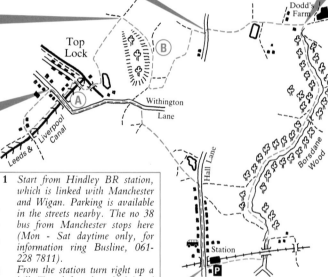

B Evidence of subsidence caused by mining can be seen all around. Buildings lean drunkenly and the land bears the scars of years of industrial activity. It is therefore pleasing to see fresh landscapes being created in the area.

Walk 5
WIGAN PIER
2 miles (3.2 km) Easy

```
0                                        1 mile
|----+----+----+----+----+----+----+----|
0                        1 km
```

Only in this century has Wigan's might as a cotton and coal producer declined. Now the town offers an excellent shopping centre, a lively museum complex on two inter-linked canalside sites and, of course, the newly reconstructed Wigan Pier: the butt of many George Formby music hall jokes. This is a fascinating walk, embracing a diversity of past industry and the transport system which made it all possible.

1 *Start from either BR's Wigan Wallgate station or from Wigan North Western station, almost opposite one another in Wallgate. The bus station is within 440 yards (400 m) and is well signposted for pedestrians. For bus information ring Busline, 061-228 7811. Parking is in nearby multi-storey car parks.*

Turn right out of North Western station or left out of Wallgate station, crossing the road. Turn right down King Street, take the third left along Rodney Street and, after crossing River Way, veer right down Harrogate Street, passing the new police station and magistrates courts on your left.

2 *Turn left along Darlington Street and fork right along Sovereign Road to join Warrington Lane. Turn right and meet the canal at Britannia Bridge, beside the Shepherds Arms pub.*

4 *Turn right and cross the canal at the next bridge, Seven Stars Bridge, and bear right into the Waterways Gardens. Continue back along the canal to the Wigan Pier Heritage Centre where you can visit a unique exhibition of local life, drink in the Orwell pub or take a waterbus trip. Return to the start along Wallgate and under the railway bridge.*

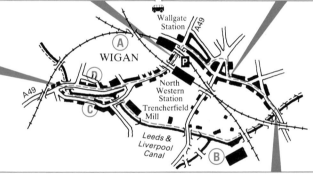

A Wigan, one of the oldest boroughs in Lancashire, has its origins in Celtic and Roman times. Throughout the middle ages it was an important market town with coal mining beginning around 1450. By the late 1800s there were over 1000 pits within the immediate area supplying some 250,000 tons of coal annually to local textile mills.

B Trencherfield Mill Engine and Machinery Hall are housed in a magnificent mill building, still in use and producing textiles. It contains the world's largest working mill engine, which is 'in steam' hourly. Old textile machinery,

3 *Turn right and follow the towpath for about 0.75 mile (1 km) to Wigan Pier Heritage Centre. Turn right just before the centre to visit Trencherfield Museum.*

Cross the canal by the foot-bridge and go ahead with the waterway on your right. Notice the newly reinstated 'Pier' and the interpretation board on the towpath.

colliery and industrial engines are also on view and working. The museum is open daily and also houses the Tourist Information Centre.

C Wigan Pier really does exist, despite eluding George Orwell on a visit in search of it. No grandiose latticework Victorian wrought-iron structure reaching out into the canal, just a diminutive hump in

the towpath to provide sufficient height for loaded coal trucks to be tipped directly into a waiting barge.

D Wigan Pier Heritage Centre, for over a hundred years the bustling centre for all the town's coal and cotton trade, is now the focus for a rather different activity: the animated portrayal of life as it was in the year 1900.

Walk 6
PENNINGTON FLASH
5 miles (8 km) Easy COUNTRY PARK

0   1 mile
0   1 km

The main feature of this surprisingly attractive walk is an expanse of water known as 'The Flash', now the focal point of Pennington Flash Country Park. Sensitive landscaping has transformed what was once referred to as 'a waste of water' into a haven for wildlife, a peaceful place for all to enjoy.

2 *Turn left by the bridge and follow a road downhill to a car park. Then take a path to your right alongside the road. Bear left on a path to cross a bridge and a stile. Follow along a hedge to cross a stile and go ahead to meet a metalled drive. Turn left to reach a road.*

1 *Start at Leigh bus station, which is well connected by bus nos 26 & 34 to Manchester (for information ring Busline, 061-228 7811). Leigh is 10 miles (16 km) west of Manchester on the A572. Roadside parking is available in the vicinity of the bus station. Turn left down King Street. Turn right at the traffic lights into Twist Lane and continue to the crossroads, where you go straight ahead. Just beyond Wigan Road on your right turn left across waste land and follow a path. After the last house fork right through some trees, then veer left to join the canal bank. Walk with the canal on your left to a concrete footbridge and cross it. Continue with the canal on your right to Plank Lane lift bridge.*

Plank Lane Bridge — A578 — **B** — Slag Lane — Leeds & Liverpool Canal — Leigh Branch — **A** — Leigh

C — Pennington Flash Country Park — Pennington Flash — Information Centre — Sorfowcow Farm — A572

3 *Turn left and go downhill, round a bend into Sandy Lane. Turn left past a sailing club car park and follow a track through a yard. Notice the waymark arrows which will lead you into the park. Continue around the lake until you reach the Information Centre.*

4 *Facing the golf course, aim for a fence on your left. Take a path to your right, then fork left over a bridge to pass a hide on your left. Fork right at the next hide, ignore a right turn and go ahead. Keep to the right and climb the steps up the canal bank. Turn right and continue to a concrete foot-bridge. Cross it and go straight ahead on a track to the road. Turn right and retrace your steps to the bus station.*

A The canal which passes through Leigh was completed in 1820. A branch of the Leeds & Liverpool Canal, it linked with the Bridgewater Canal, thus making a through route to Manchester.

B The site of Bickershaw Colliery is a reminder that this was once an important mining area of the South Lancashire coalfield. The extraction of coal used to be a slow process, being removed from the mines by pit ponies pulling bogies. Wagonways were connected with the Leeds & Liverpool Canal where horse-drawn barges transported the coal to the industrial towns.

C It was the introduction of deep mining techniques which brought about the subsidence of the surrounding area and the appearance of the flash, or lake. Arable land, farms and railways have all been slowly swallowed up by the the rising flood waters. Now a peaceful habitat for over 200 bird species, Pennington Flash was awarded Country Park status in 1978.

THE MANCHESTER, BOLTON & BURY CANAL

2.5 miles (4 km) Easy

0 — 1 mile
0 — 1 km

A disused canal, two reservoirs and several small dairy farms combine to offer both variety and tranquillity. Although Radcliffe lies trapped in the cleft of two intersecting motorways, this walk offers open views towards the Pennines and follows a route well beyond the traffic's roar.

4 *Turn right and follow a rough track towards a distant farm. Skirt the buildings to turn right downhill towards the reservoir. Keeping the reservoir on your left, follow the track to some farm buildings and a large house on your right. Continue downhill to meet the canal again at 'Benny's Nightclub'.*

3 *Turn left. After 50 yards (45m) turn right over a stile to follow the perimeter of the cemetery on your right. Cross a stile and go ahead down a field with the hedge on your left. Climb a gate, go through a farmyard and then walk uphill along a concrete roadway towards some houses.*

2 *Turn right and then left to cross the canal on a disused railway bridge. Follow the path between the abutments of a dismantled railway bridge uphill towards a farm, ignoring a fork to the left. Go through a gate, cross the farmyard and follow a track straight ahead to the cemetery railings, ignoring the left fork.*

5 *Turn right and follow the track across the canal to join the towpath at the end of a stone slab wall. Walk along the towpath with the canal on your right for about 1.25 miles (2 km) until you reach the point where you earlier crossed on the the disused railway bridge. Turn left and retrace your steps to the station.*

1 *Start from Radcliffe BR station, which is on the Manchester to Bury line and interconnects with the Supertram. There is a regular bus service from Manchester and Bury (for information ring Busline, 061-228 7811) and car parking at the station (charge). Go diagonally across the station car park to cross a road and join a footpath to the left of a school. Go ahead until you meet the canal.*

A Elton Reservoir, completed in 1805, was built to provide a plentiful supply of water for the top pound of the nearby canal. Supplied by a feeder canal from the River Irwell, nearly 3 miles (4.8 km) away, it covers an area of 54 acres (22 hectares) and holds 150 million gallons (680 million litres).

B The Manchester, Bolton & Bury Canal, officially closed in 1961, once linked the towns from which it derives its name. Leaving the River Irwell in Salford it climbs northwards for 8 miles (13 km) to Prestolee where it divides: one arm going to Bolton and the other to Bury, via Radcliffe; in all a total of 15 miles (24 km). Completed in 1796, the waterway prospered initially on its coal trade. Other industries then grew up along its banks, including chemicals, cotton mills, dye works and timber yards. In Radcliffe, once the centre of the coloured weaving industry before mechanisation, the canalside is still dominated by weaving mills.

Once closed, it looked as though the canal would gradually be infilled, with new development completely obliterating the line in places. However, in July 1987 a society was formed with the object of preserving the canal and ultimately restoring it to full navigable standard.

Walk 8

WORSLEY DELPH &

5 miles (8 km) Easy **THE BARTON SWING AQUEDUCT**

This is a fascinating exploration of waterways history, combining a walk along the Bridgewater Canal, the first canal of 'the canal age', with a close up view of the Manchester Ship canal, the last major canal to be built in this country. Each was a magnificent feat of engineering in its time.

1 Start at Patricroft BR station on the Manchester to Liverpool line. There is a regular bus service from Manchester (for information ring Busline, 061-228 7811) and parking in adjacent side streets.
Turn left out of the station and, after the road bends left opposite the hospital, turn right along New Street. Turn left opposite the Red Lion pub and cross the main road to continue to the end of Cawdor Street. Turn right along Trafford Road and right again at the junction with Barton Lane. Go under the aqueduct to turn left along Barton Road and cross the Manchester Ship Canal. Notice the Barton Swing Aqueduct on your left.

2 Turn left along Chapel Place and bear left along a brick path to take a flight of steps onto the canal bank. View the aqueduct and the ship canal. Retrace your steps to the Barton Road/Barton Lane cross roads and go ahead to join the canal towpath on your right. Follow the canal back through Patricroft out into the open countryside on your right, and then into Worsley to a junction in front of a timber framed black and white building.

3 From the Packet House follow the path along the canal and up onto Worsley Road to turn right. Go ahead to Drywood Avenue keeping The Crescent and village green on your right. Turn right through a housing estate to rejoin the canal and walk back to Patricroft.

4 When the path leaves the canal beside a lodge, turn left and then immediately right along Canal Bank Road. Bear right at the junction with Green Lane and go ahead to return to the station.

Bear left under a bridge, then left again up some stone steps to cross the road and descend back to the canal and the black and white Packet House.

A The Manchester Ship Canal, a 36 mile (58 km) cut linking Manchester to the Mersey Estuary, was begun in 1887 and completed in 1894. Coal brought into the city from the Duke of Bridgewater's Worsley mines over 100 years earlier had successfully fuelled the fires of Manchester's industrial revolution. It was, however, the rich merchants of Liverpool who appeared to be deriving most benefit by charging high docking fees, both for shipping in raw materials and for exporting the finished goods. They held the key to the Mersey which was not navigable to ocean-going shipping beyond Warrington. The solution

Over

lay in turning the River Irwell, a treacherous river linking Manchester to the Mersey, into a 120 feet (37 m) wide by 28 feet (9 m) deep canal. This alleviated the previously regular flooding, especially in Salford, and swallowed the waters of four of its tributaries, the rivers Irk, Roach and Medlock, and the Corn Brook.

Shipping of up to 12,500 tons could now steam into the heart of Manchester and berth beside the factories of Trafford Park or on the other side at the busy Pomona Docks. Sadly, the canal has seen a steady decline in the traffic handled over the last 25 years with the terminal docks closed at Manchester except for part of 9 Dock. The area has been developed into what is now known as Salford Quays, comprising office developments and housing.

Worsley Delph, on the Bridgewater Canal

B The impressive wrought-iron construction of the Barton Swing Aqueduct, completed in 1894, replaced an equally magnificent fixed structure built by Brindley some 130 years earlier. The original aqueduct, built of stone, was a most elegant structure and carried the Bridgewater Canal over the River Irwell. Initially the idea that boats could 'be floated over a bridge across a river' was ridiculed and Brindley became the subject of scorn. Later it was to be described as the eighth wonder of the world. The present swing aqueduct was designed by Sir Edward Leader Williams, a tank 235 feet (72 m) long by 18 feet (5.5 m) wide and 7 feet (2 m) deep, capable of being swung at right angles to the ship canal. The entire structure is operated full of water and weighs a total of 1,450 tons (1,473,200 kg). It has no towpath.

C Worsley Delph can rightly be described as the birthplace of commercial canals in Britain. On 23rd March 1759 Francis Egerton, third Duke of Bridgewater, received the royal assent to construct an artificial waterway from his Worsley mines to Salford in Manchester. On its completion six years later the canal revolutionised transport in this country by allowing one horse towing a barge to move up to 500 times as much as a loaded pack horse. In so doing the Duke also opened up the way for the burgeoning industrial revolution. Whilst the canal was under construction a system of underground waterways was being built, on several different levels and linked by ingenious inclined planes, throughout the mines. In this way coal could be floated directly from the working face deep in the mine to consumers in the heart of Manchester, using narrow double-ended boats known as 'starvationers'. Some 50 miles (80 km) of underground waterways were eventually constructed and remained in use until the late 19th century. The name 'Delph' comes from the old English 'delved place' and refers to the quarry close to the mine entrances used as the source of the sandstone employed in the construction of the canal.

DUNHAM MASSEY PARK

3.5 miles (5.6 km) Easy

0   1 mile
0   1 km

Dunham Massey is a rare and important example of a formal 18th-century park, making this walk, which takes you through it, a rewarding experience. The splendid house is also well worth visiting – but note that it is closed on Fridays. Observe the notices regarding dogs in the Deer Park.

1 *Start from the National Trust car park (charge; closes at 6.30 pm) at Dunham Massey Hall. This is clearly signposted off the A56 near Altrincham. Bus no 38 between Warrington & Altrincham stops at the entrance (for information ring Cheshire Bus, 0925 444250).*
From the entrance, walk to your left, passing under the canal. Turn left over a stile to walk with the canal on your left. Continue over the River Bollin Aqueduct.

6 *Cross the canal bridge, turn right down the path to join the canal. Go under the bridge and walk with the canal on your left. Continue under one bridge. Just after the concrete underbridge, turn right to cross a stile and rejoin the road. Turn right to return to the start.*

5 *When you reach a signpost, turn right for Oldfield Lane. Cross a stile, walk ahead along the lane for about 20 yards (18 m), then cross a stile by a gate to your left. Walk across the field to a signpost. Turn left along the path to School Lane. Cross a stile and join the road. Turn right, passing the church on your left.*

4 *You emerge on a golf course – BEWARE of flying golf balls! Walk ahead across a fairway, then veer slightly left, passing the 18th tee on your left. When you come to the end of an old fence on your right, turn left to walk across more fairways, between obvious gaps in trees. Cross the stile ahead, and continue.*

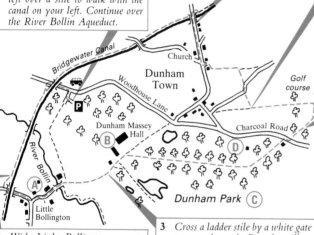

The garden has been restored and replanted and contains an Edwardian water garden, an Elizabethan mount and an Orangery. In the Coach House there is an audio-visual display of the history of Dunham Massey. Owned by the National Trust, the Hall is open 1 - 5 pm daily except Fri (Sun & B. Hols 12 - 5 pm) Apr - Oct. The mill operates on Weds in summer. Charge.

C There are 150 fallow deer roaming freely within 230 acres of parkland, notable for its formal avenues of trees. These are arranged in a 'goosefoot' pattern, radiating from the hall.

D This red brick building is the deer barn, built in 1740.

2 *With Little Bollington over to your left, and the parapet of the next underbridge about 30 yards (27 m) ahead, walk down steps on your right. Turn left at a lane to walk under the canal. Turn left at a road, passing The Swan With Two Nicks pub on your left. Continue ahead, crossing a footbridge and walking along a path between fences.*

3 *Cross a ladder stile by a white gate to enter the park. Pass the mill on your left. In front of the Hall, the drives split. Take the right hand fork and continue. Leave the park by a white ladder stile. Cross the road and walk about 15 yards (14 m) to the right, then take a narrow path through trees on your left.*

A Here you pass the Swan With Two Nicks pub. The nicks refer to marks made on the beak when 'swan upping', or counting.

B Dunham Massey Hall was for over 300 years the seat of the Earls of Stamford and Warrington. There are 30 richly furnished rooms to see, with fine collections of furniture, portraits and silver.

Walk 10

LYMM

3.5 miles (5.6 km) Easy

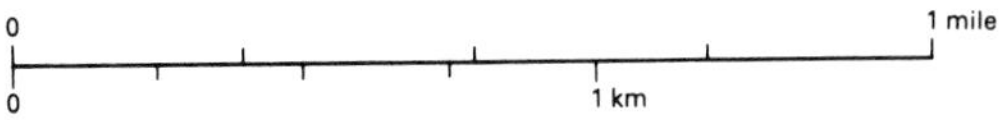

The ancient village of Lymm is a welcoming place, its old streets and buildings inviting exploration. This walk begins in the village centre, then diverts via the historic Bridgewater Canal to the fine woods at Lymm Dam. If you listen carefully, you will hear the friendly chimes of the church clock all the way around.

1 *Lymm is on the A56 & B5158, signposted off the M6 and M56 near where they cross. Follow directions to the village centre. You will see a car park behind the old village cross. Bus nos 37 & 38 between Warrington and Altrincham stop here (for infor- mation ring Cheshire Bus, 0925 444250).*
In front of the cross are the stocks. With these behind you, walk to the right to cross the canal bridge. Turn right to join the towpath and walk with the canal on your right.

2 *Leave the canal just before Lloyd bridge, the first you reach. Cross the bridge and turn right along the bridleway signposted to Lymm. You emerge at a road, then pass a school to your left. Turn left along Orchard Avenue.*

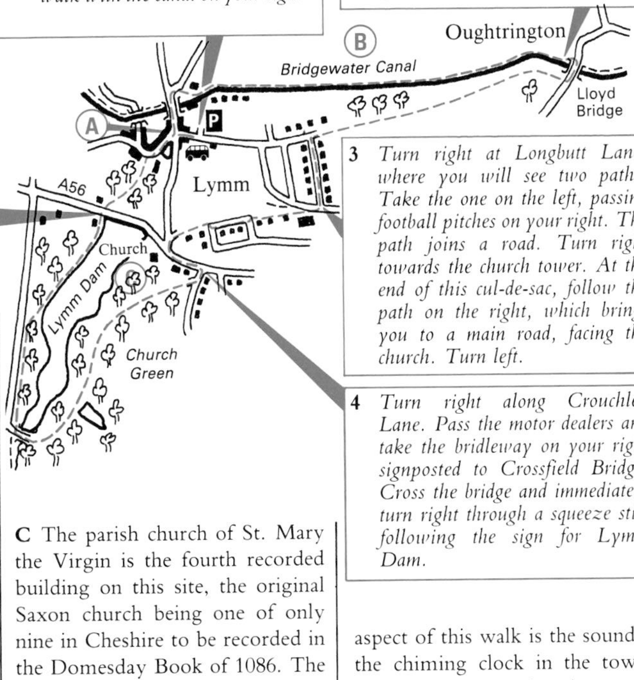

5 *Cross the main road beside the dam and follow the path opposite, down steps and through trees. Emerge at a road by a small lake. Turn right along The Cross to return to the start.*

A Lymm Cross, standing on a rock outcrop in the middle of a cobbled square, dates from the 17th century. The stocks at its base are a modern replica of the original set.

B When the canal came to Lymm in the mid 18th century, the village was saved from the worst excesses of the industrial revolution by the lack of coal and soft water in this area. Easier access to Manchester did give a boost to the existing local industry, however, and the manufacture of fustian, a thick twilled short-napped cotton cloth usually dyed dark, thrived. The canal wharf, where these goods were loaded, can be seen beside the bridge. It is now the base of the Lymm Cruising Club.

3 *Turn right at Longbutt Lane, where you will see two paths. Take the one on the left, passing football pitches on your right. The path joins a road. Turn right towards the church tower. At the end of this cul-de-sac, follow the path on the right, which brings you to a main road, facing the church. Turn left.*

4 *Turn right along Crouchley Lane. Pass the motor dealers and take the bridleway on your right signposted to Crossfield Bridge. Cross the bridge and immediately turn right through a squeeze stile following the sign for Lymm Dam.*

C The parish church of St. Mary the Virgin is the fourth recorded building on this site, the original Saxon church being one of only nine in Cheshire to be recorded in the Domesday Book of 1086. The next, built by the Normans, probably lasted until 1320, when a third church was erected. The present building dates from 1851, with the tower being reconstructed in 1889. A tomb canopy in the south aisle dates from the 14th century. A particularly charming aspect of this walk is the sound of the chiming clock in the tower, which can be heard each quarter-hour as you travel round. This been a feature of St. Mary's since 1690, when entries for *oyle for ye clocke and belles* first appear in the church records. The clock you now see was gifted to the church in 1891, and was electrified in 1966.

Map labels: Oughtrington, Bridgewater Canal, Lloyd Bridge, Lymm, A56, Church, Lymm Dam, Church Green, B, A, P

DARESBURY

3.5 miles (5.6 km) Easy

0   1 mile
0   1 km

A varied and fascinating walk offering sweeping views over the Mersey estuary. It starts from the village of Daresbury, a haven of peace beside a busy road and a motorway. The scholar, children's author and poet Charles Lutwidge Dodgson, 'Lewis Carroll', was born close by, and his father was the vicar here. Daresbury church has a Lewis Carroll memorial window, which you can arrange to see.

3 At Moore Bridge cross the canal and follow Hobb Lane to the main road. Cross the road carefully to the stile in the fence.

4 Climb the stile and walk ahead across the field for 175 yards (160 m). Then turn right to walk with woods on your right. Cross a stile and turn left immediately to walk around the edge of the field to a stile beside a gate. Cross the stile and walk along Hall Lane.

5 Go through a gateway and turn right at Daresbury Lane to walk back to the village, passing the church on your right.

1 Start from the Ring o' Bells pub in Daresbury. The village is just off the A56, a short distance from junction 11 on the M56. Roadside parking is easy, and bus no C30 between Chester and Warrington stops by the pub (for information ring Cheshire Bus, 0925 444250).
With your back to the Ring o' Bells, walk to the right along the road. Fork right along a lane to the right of a lawn mower repair shop, and continue on grass to a large tree. Bear right to cross a stile at the main road.

2 Carefully cross this busy road. Climb over the stile directly opposite and follow the path. Cross another stile, then follow the path signposted to Delph Lane, entering Daresbury Firs. Follow the obvious path through fir trees, crossing a green track, to come to a stile beside a gate. Cross it and continue along a headland path which shortly bends left to join a road. Turn right, cross the canal bridge and turn immediately right to walk with the canal on your right.

A These buildings are the Daresbury Laboratories, where the government conducts science and engineering research.

B Charles Lutwidge Dodgson (1832-98), 'Lewis Carroll', was born and grew up at the Old Parsonage, Newton-by-Daresbury, some 2 miles (3.2 km) south of All Saints Church, Daresbury (pronounced Darzbry), where his father was vicar. The Old Parsonage burned down in 1883, and was never rebuilt, although a plaque in the middle of a field, with a quotation from Carroll's poem *The Three Sunsets*, marks the spot. All Saints has a pretty memorial window to the famous author, made in 1934 and depicting Lewis Carroll with characters from *Alice's Adventures in Wonderland*. Viewing is by prior appointment – ring 0925 740348.

Walk 12

SALTERSFORD & BARNTON TUNNELS

5 miles (8.0 km) Easy

An outward walk along a very rural stretch of the Trent & Mersey Canal ends with a visit to two fine old canal tunnels and splendid views over Saltersford Locks. You then descend to river level for the return along a remote and peaceful valley. This route links with Walk 13 at point **1**.

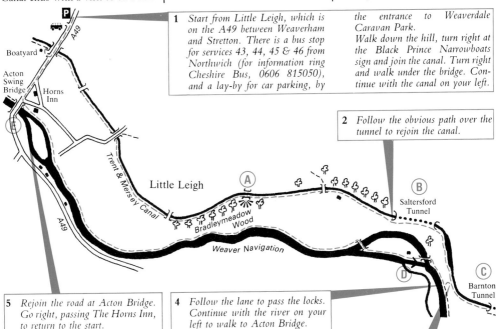

1 *Start from Little Leigh, which is on the A49 between Weaverham and Stretton. There is a bus stop for services 43, 44, 45 & 46 from Northwich (for information ring Cheshire Bus, 0606 815050), and a lay-by for car parking, by the entrance to Weaverdale Caravan Park. Walk down the hill, turn right at the Black Prince Narrowboats sign and join the canal. Turn right and walk under the bridge. Continue with the canal on your left.*

2 *Follow the obvious path over the tunnel to rejoin the canal.*

5 *Rejoin the road at Acton Bridge. Go right, passing The Horns Inn, to return to the start.*

4 *Follow the lane to pass the locks. Continue with the river on your left to walk to Acton Bridge.*

3 *Where the canal narrows after a wide stretch, note a tarmac lane leading downhill to the river. Walk on to see the entrance to Barnton Tunnel, then return to this lane and turn left to walk down to the river.*

A There is a good view over the Weaver valley from this small stone aqueduct.

B Saltersford Tunnel is 424 yards (388 m) long. Due to a surveyor's miscalculation, it was built crooked. Look out for the circular brick ventilation shaft to the left of the path as you walk over the top.

C Barnton Tunnel is 573 yards (524 m) long. You can see light at the other end from the towpath, and, if you are lucky, the bright headlight of a narrowboat chugging towards you.

D Only the largest of the paired Saltersford Locks is in regular use. It raises the level of the navigation 7 feet 3 inches (2.2 m).

E Acton Swing Bridge was built in 1933 and weighs 650 tons (650,000 kg). When it swings open, most of its weight is carried by a floating pontoon, so it only requires a minimal amount of electricity to power it.

23

Walk 13
DUTTON LOCKS
7.5 miles (12 km) Moderate

The Trent & Mersey Canal is followed on the initial part of this route. Delightfully rural, the waterway contours along the hillside about 60 feet (18 m) above the River Weaver, before plunging into Preston Brook Tunnel. After a visit to the traditional canal scene around the tunnel entrance, you then go cross-country to the impressive Dutton Locks. From there, rich farmland, woods and pretty cottages are explored as you complete this circular walk. This route can be linked with Walk 12 at point 1.

A This is an excellent example of an original Trent & Mersey canal milepost, bearing the foundry mark 'R & D Stone 1819'. Many of these went missing over the years, but all the gaps have now been filled by the Trent & Mersey Canal Society. The replacements can be identified by the foundry mark 'T & MCS 1977'.

B A charming canal scene around the southern portal of Preston Brook Tunnel. A dry dock is still in use, its ornate bargeboards and slender cast iron columns painted tastefully. It is usually surrounded by a variety of narrowboats, often including working boats, distinguished by their tarpaulin covers.

The lock here is a stop lock. It wasn't built to change the level of the canal, but to protect one canal company's water from being 'stolen' by another. A boat passing through a normal narrow lock uses about 25,000 gallons (113,650 litres) of water, which passes down the canal from the summit level, and has to be continually topped up from rivers, streams and reservoirs. This made canal water a resource to be guarded jealously.

Preston Brook Tunnel is 1239 yards (1133 m) long, eighth in the league of long navigable canal tunnels in the UK. It is crooked, like Saltersford Tunnel (also on the Trent & Mersey Canal, see Walk 12), and has no towpath through it. The path taken by the canal horses over the top still exists and can be followed easily. While the horses took this route, the boat would be 'legged' through, the crew lying on their backs on the boat and walking it through against the tunnel wall.

C The present Dutton Locks date from 1874, when a large ship lock was built alongside the old barge lock, to cope with increased traffic. This new lock could accommodate a steam packet and its tow of three dumb barges in one locking. Originally the gates were operated by water turbines, which are still in position under cast iron covers on the island between the locks. An electro-hydraulic system replaced the old machinery in 1979.

The biggest ship to pass through was the *St. Michael* from the Netherlands, with a length of 208 feet and a beam of 33 feet (63 x 10 m). Vessels from as far away as Antigua and Singapore have used these locks, on their way upstream to the ICI chemical works at Winnington. The river is tidal to Dutton Locks on high spring tides. Sluices beyond the lock-side buildings are used to control the river flow in times of spate.

These massive river locks provide a stark contrast with the diminutive stop lock at **B**.

D The main west coast electric railway crosses the river on Dutton Viaduct, a towering structure built in 1834.

E Acton Swing Bridge was built in 1933 and weighs 650 tons (650,000 kg). When it swings open, most of its weight is carried by a floating pontoon, so it only requires a minimal amount of electricity to power it.

Over

3 Continue along the tarmac track. Where a fork to the left crosses a cattle grid, go straight ahead for 20 yards (18 m), then follow a bridleway sign on your left, crossing grass to a bridle-gate. Go through and follow the track, keeping a ditch to your left. Ahead you will see a large white foot-bridge. Follow the path to this, through two gates. Cross the bridge and walk to the locks.

4 Cross the locks to a stile. Cross this and walk up the field to go through a gate. Turn right and go over a stile beside a gate, then follow the track past Manor Farm, climbing three stiles to reach a T-junction. Turn right to go under the railway. After 60 yards (55 m) turn left up an ungated track, ignoring a stile and footpath sign beside it. Follow the track round to the right. Cross a stile beside a gate, cross a field and, by the corner of a fence, follow a narrow path downhill to a foot-bridge. Cross it and another stile, and continue ahead for about 100 yards (90 m).

5 Turn left to follow a track over a ditch, and go on to join the road at a gate. Turn left. After 400 yards (365 m) take a track to the left. Then 30 yards (27 m) further on turn right over a stile by a gate. Walk to the left of a prominent tree, downhill to a little foot-bridge. Cross it. Follow the path to a second foot-bridge and cross it. Go through a wooden gate, turn left immediately and follow the path uphill. This soon becomes a track. Turn right just before the railway bridge and continue.

2 A footpath sign and stile after bridge 213 indicate a path to your left. You will return to this point. Continue along the towpath to view the tunnel entrance, then return to the stile and cross it. Follow the direction of the sign across a grassy field to join a road at a stile. Turn right and follow the road to pass Dutton Lodge Farm on your right.

1 Start from Little Leigh, which is on the A49 between Weaverham and Stretton. There is a bus stop for services 43, 44, 45 & 46 from Northwich (for information ring Cheshire Bus, 0606 815050), and a lay-by for car parking, by the entrance to Weaverdale Caravan Park.
Walk down the hill, turn right at the Black Prince Narrowboats sign and join the canal. Walk with the canal on your right.

6 Climb a stile by a gate and cross the bridge over the railway. Follow the track to the road. Turn left and follow this road to the A49. Turn left to walk over the swing bridge and back to the start.

Preston Brook Tunnel

B

Longacre Wood

Dutton Lodge Farm

Island Farm

A

C

Dutton Locks

D

Manor Farm

Dutton Viaduct

Trent & Mersey Canal

Weaver Navigation

Boatyard

Horns Inn

Acton Swing Bridge

E

Acton Bridge

A49

Danes Gutter

Yew Tree Farm

Poplar Farm

P

0   1 mile
0   1 km

Walk 14
MARBURY COUNTRY PARK
4 miles (6.4 km) Easy   **& THE ANDERTON BOAT LIFT**

0   1 mile
0   1 km

Budworth Mere, The Big Wood and their associated wildlife are unique attractions in an area as industrialised as this, and they get the walk off to a fine start. This high standard is maintained along a length of the Trent & Mersey Canal which meanders in rural isolation until the magnificent Anderton Boat Lift is reached, and the industry alongside the River Weaver is seen in the valley below. The return is made via a pleasant walk across fields. This route can be linked with Walk **15** at point **2**.

5 *Cross the stile 25 yards (23 m) beyond the last house on the right and follow the path, climbing three stiles, before crossing the hedge by another stile. Walk across a field to a stile at Coggeshall Lane. Cross this and the stile opposite. Beyond the next two stiles you enter woods. Cross a foot-bridge and another two stiles to reach a road.*

6 *Turn right. Walk along the road, forking left to Marbury Country Park where signposted. Turn left to return to the car park, or continue with the walk if you have arrived by bus.*

1 *Start from the car park (which closes at 7pm) at Marbury Country Park. This is well signposted from the swing bridge on the A533 at Anderton. Those arriving by bus no 46 from Northwich BR station (for information ring Cheshire Bus, 0606 815050) should start the walk at point **3**.*
From the car park, walk past the Information Centre on your left, following signs for The Mere. Turn right at The Mere and walk beside the water to the slipway, where you turn right. Now follow signs to the canal. When you reach the canal, walk with it on your left through the woods to the road.

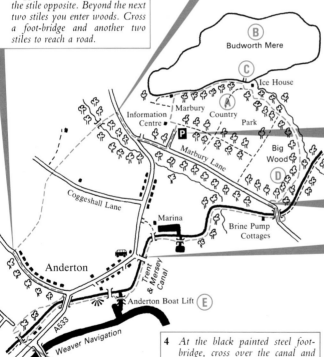

2 *Turn left at the road, walk over the canal bridge and down steps on your left to the towpath (you can link with Walk **15** here). Now walk under the bridge with the canal on your right. Those who arrived by bus should return to the bus stop at bridge 199.*

3 *Those arriving by bus start the walk from the stop by Anderton Post Office. Cross the canal bridge opposite, and walk along the towpath with the canal on your right.*

4 *At the black painted steel foot-bridge, cross over the canal and walk up the zigzag concrete path. At the top, follow the path to the right, with houses on your left. Walk through woods. At the next bridge, walk up to the road and turn sharp left along Hough Lane.*

Over

MARBURY COUNTRY PARK & THE ANDERTON BOAT LIFT
Continued

A Marbury Country Park has been created in what were the grounds of Marbury Hall, a grand house in the style of the French palace of Fontainbleau. Marbury Hall was built, it is said, to alleviate the homesickness of James Hugh Smith Barry's French wife. Completed in the 1840s, it was pulled down in 1968 when it had deteriorated beyond repair.

The landscape gardener John Nesfield created the park while the house was being built, and, as you walk down to the Mere, you will see formal avenues of lime trees to your right, part of his grand design.

B The large expanse of Budworth Mere attracts a variety of birds, with reeds and trees at the water's edge providing food and shelter. Of the many varieties of birds found here, a colony of reed warblers are of particular note, as they are living at the extreme north-western edge of their range. Secretive birds which hide in the reeds, you may hear them: their song sounds like two pebbles being tapped together.

Great crested grebes also congregate here during spring, along with many of the usual species of waterfowl and swans.

C The slipway was built to enable the Smith Barrys to go by boat to the church at Great Budworth, where they had a private chapel.

By the path as you walk away from the slipway are the remains of an ice house, where ice taken in winter from the pond nearby was stored for summer use. The domed roof is gone, but the lined pit where the ice was packed in straw for insulation, remains.

D The Big Wood was planted in the 1850s as part of Nesfield's plan, and explains the wide variety of trees to be seen here: oak, sycamore and beech alongside more exotic species such as the Chilean pine, or monkey puzzle tree, and Portuguese larch. In spring time the ground is carpeted with bluebells, wood-sorrel and wood anenome.

Bird life in the wood is prolific, and includes many of the woodland species such as nuthatch, tree creeper, greater and lesser spotted woodpecker, wren, tawny owl, whitethroat and siskin. A complete list is available at the Information Centre. Grey squirrels are all around. Less likely to be seen, although they are here, are foxes, rabbits, weasels and wood mice.

E Regarded as one of the 'seven wonders of the waterways', the Anderton Boat Lift is an impressive piece of machinery, built in 1875 to allow the passage of boats between the Trent & Mersey Canal and the River Weaver 50 feet 4 inches (15.3 m) below.

Prior to the building of the lift, goods were transhipped using chutes and inclined lifts, a laborious task. A steady increase in trade required that a more efficient system be created, and Edward Leader Williams (later engineer of the Manchester Ship Canal) was employed to design the lift.

His creation enabled boats to be floated into tanks, which were then sealed with water-tight doors. By adjusting the amount of water in each tank, the top one would gently lower, causing the bottom one to rise, using a system of hydraulic rams. The apparent elegant simplicity of this mechanism belied the mechanical difficulties involved. Constant problems resulted in a system of wire ropes and pulleys, operating on counterbalances with the aid of a small electric motor, being installed in 1908. Each tank then operated independently, and this is how it remains today.

During the late 1980s a massive overhaul of the lift was begun, and there are firm plans to revitalise the whole site, as recently discovered cargo chutes, tramways, cobbled walkways and engine installations will provide sufficient added interest to develop the area around the lift into a major attraction. The historical significance of the Anderton Boat Lift has resulted in its designation as an ancient monument.

Walk 15

NEUMANN'S FLASH & THE LION SALT WORKS

4.5 miles (7.2 km) Easy

Rock salt was laid down in Cheshire during the Triassic period 190 - 225 million years ago. Where natural ground water breaches two underground salt beds it forms brine streams, and the Romans used these, where they surfaced, as natural brine springs. Large scale exploitation around Northwich began in 1670 when prospectors, digging for coal, discovered salt. Construction of the River Weaver Navigation and the Trent & Mersey Canal made the transportation of coal and salt much less expensive, enabling this natural resource to be realised fully. Modern chemical works located in this area have their origins in the salt industry, which has left an indelible mark on the countryside around Northwich, although time and a great deal of landscaping has healed most of the scars. On this walk you will enjoy fine countryside alongside what visible remains there are. Walk 14 links with this route at point 3 – as the Lion Salt Works is only open to visitors during the afternoon, why not do Walk 14 during the morning, followed by this walk in the afternoon?

A Neumann's and Ashton's Flashes (a local word for lakes) were formed by the subsidence of old salt mines. Ashton's, now completely dry, is likely to be used for landfill, but the small wildfowl lake, all that now remains of Neumann's Flash, is to be preserved, with the surrounding area planted with trees.

B The canal embankment here offers an expansive view over the surrounding farmland. The tall and conspicuous church tower is in the village of Great Budworth.

C The Lion Salt Works date from 1842, when the Thompson family began pumping wild brine from 150 feet (46 m) below ground. The brine was evaporated in iron pans to produce crystal and lump salt. Heavily dependent on exports to West Africa, the works closed in 1986 when this market collapsed. Luckily, Vale Royal Council recognised the importance of this, the last remaining factory, and purchased it to avoid demolition. There is now an active restoration project in hand, a visitor centre has been established and the whole complex is well worth visiting.

The slatted wooden building by the canal bridge is the salt store, built in 1901 and known as the Coronation Store. Loading doors opened directly onto the towpath. The visitor centre, shop and museum are housed in the old Red Lion Inn, which was converted from two terraced cottages built in 1877. Extended at the rear, it became a lodging house in 1940, and offices for the works in 1950. Other houses in the terrace were demolished due to subsidence caused by salt workings, a common occurrence in Marston.

Within the works is the steam engine, standing alongside the bore holes. A 'nodding donkey' beam pump kept the big black brine tank, which stands by the canal, topped up. This fed all the evaporating pans. It was in these pans that the brine was boiled, using coal, then later, oil, to form salt crystals. These were raked to the side and shovelled into tubs by the lumpman. The rectangular blocks of salt thus formed were then dried for two weeks in the Stove House, before being kept in the store ready for sale.

Complete restoration of this important site will take some time, but it is hoped that eventually salt will once again be produced here by the open pan method. Usually open daily 1.30 - 4.30 pm (by volunteer effort) – telephone 0606 40555 to check.

D The industry which brought prosperity to Marston also contributed, literally, to its downfall. Gaps in terraces of houses are the visible manifestation of constant subsidence caused by the removal of salt and rock on a massive scale. Mines flooded regularly, the canal sank continuously and breached spectacularly in 1907, and smoke and ash from the salt works caused pollution on a grand scale. In spite of this the village enjoyed international recognition. One of the most notable visitors was the Czar of Russia who, in 1844, enjoyed a candle-lit supper 340 feet (104 m) underground in the Adelaide Mine.

Over

NEUMANN'S FLASH

Continued   **& THE LION SALT WORKS**

0   1 mile

0   1 km

4   *At bridge 193, by the slatted wooden salt store, turn right to join the road. About 60 yards (55 m) along on your left, enter The* **Lion Salt Works.** *Rejoin the canal by the large black brine tank and continue walking with the canal on your left.*

5   *Turn right immediately after bridge 191. Join a track and turn left, passing G Cross & Sons to your right and crossing a stile. Continue with a fence on your left. When the fence turns sharp left at a corner, continue ahead, down a rough path through bushes. Cross a new stile beside an old gate, turn left and follow a clear track which doubles back to the right. Go over a foot-bridge and continue ahead to the main road. Turn right. Fork left at Tesco's to return to the station.*

3   *Just before the canal bridge, turn right down the steps to the towpath (you can link with Walk* **14** *here). Walk with the canal on your left.*

2   *Where the road bends to the left, there are the remains of a wire gate on your right. Walk through the woods here to overlook Neumann's Flash, then return to the road. Turn right and continue along the road.*

1   *Start from Northwich BR station, which is on the Manchester (Oxford Road) to Chester line. Many buses stop here (for information ring Cheshire Bus, 0606 815050), and there is a car park. From the station entrance, walk past the Lion & Railway pub and along Station Road, veering right* *to the roundabout. Cross carefully to the other side of the roundabout to Leicester Street. Walk along the side of this street and turn right at the first crossroads. Walk over Witton Mill Bridge and continue with an embankment on your right.*

Marbury Country Park

Trent & Mersey Canal

Marston

Lion Salt Works

Wincham

Witton Brook

Neumann's Flash

B5075

Ashton's Flash

A559

A559

NORTHWICH

Station

29

Walk 16
LITTLEBOROUGH
5 miles (8.0 km) Moderate

A bracing walk on open moorland alongside Chelburn reservoirs provides a good vantage point from which to view a typical Pennine landscape. As the Rochdale Canal makes its way, lock by lock, towards the summit, the railway disappears into a tunnel in the hillside below.

2 Cross a canal bridge, go straight ahead uphill and follow the sign to Lydgate. Go through a gate and follow a waymarked track. Just above the reservoir follow the sign left to Lydgate over the moor. Join a stream and follow a path uphill to a high stone wall. Climb a stile and continue towards a stone cottage.

1 Start from Littleborough BR station, which is on the Manchester to York line. Littleborough is on the A58, 3 miles (4.8 km) northeast of Rochdale. Regular buses stop nearby (for information ring Busline, 061-228 7811) and you may park at the station.
Go through the pedestrian tunnel under the railway and turn left. Where the road bends left go straight on to join the canal. Continue along the towpath. Notice the entrance to the railway tunnel on your left just beyond the last of the Courtauld factories. Go ahead until you reach West Summit Lock no 37 (there is a clear sign in the wall of the canalside house).

3 Join an unmetalled road by the stone cottage. Go ahead 100 yards (90m) and turn right to cross a stile and follow a stone wall on your left towards the reservoir. At the bottom of the field squeeze through a gap, turn left and follow a stream with a wall on your right. Turn right at the second gateway and aim for a stile. Continue towards a farm house. Climb a stile, cross the farmyard and continue on down the drive.

4 At the end of the drive turn left over a bridge, continue for 50 yards (45m), then go left up a path at a signpost to Lydgate. Cross a road, go over a stile and continue on the path. Turn left onto a road then right onto a public footpath.

5 Go diagonally left to a gate. Pass through and continue straight ahead with a wall on your right. Cross a stile, a stream and another stile. Alongside a cottage go through a lychgate and follow the edge of a golf course with a boundary fence on your left. Descend to cross a stream. Go through a kissing-gate and turn right onto a road. Follow the road round to your right by a row of cottages, to cross the canal. Turn left, then left again along Canal Street, to return to the station.

B When Summit Tunnel was opened in 1839, it was the longest railway tunnel in the world, being 2869 yards (2625 m) long. In 1984 a goods train carrying petroleum caught fire in the tunnel causing flames to belch uncontrollably from the ventilation shafts for several weeks.

A The Rochdale Canal spans 33 miles (53 km) across the Pennines. Its climb to the summit, 600 feet (180 m) above sea level, involves 56 locks to the west and 36 to the east.

30

Walk 17

TODMORDEN

3 miles (4.8 km) Easy

0   1 mile

0   1 km

On the pediment of Todmorden's grand Town Hall ten figures toil away at the town's three principal industries: cotton, wool and agriculture. This walk takes in facets of all three and follows a section of the Rochdale Canal which served them all, and helped them prosper. As you leave the canal, you will enjoy a splendid view over Todmorden and the valleys beyond.

3 *Leave the canal at the third bridge, beside a derelict mill. Cross the bridge and follow the road uphill. In the middle of a row of cottages, fork left up a waymarked track signed for the Calderdale Way (yellow arrow).*

When the track swings left, go straight ahead ignoring the waymark arrow. Maintain your direction following the path which climbs along the side of the hill. Go ahead through a large gap in a stone wall.

2 *Follow the towpath with the canal on your right. High on the hill ahead you can see Stoodley Pike monument.*

1 *Start from the BR station at Todmorden, where cars can be parked. Bus nos 589 & 590 run from Rochdale and stop close to the point where the walk joins the canal (for bus information ring 0422 364467).*
Go down Rise Lane to the right of the Queen Hotel and turn right along Rochdale Road to meet the canal. Turn right onto the towpath and then left to pass under the road bridge beside a lock.

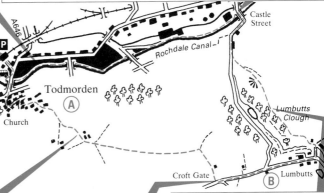

6 *Go ahead, downhill, to some houses. Maintaining your direction, descend a series of steps linking the parallel streets and rows of houses. Turn left along Bank Street heading towards the church and rejoin Rochdale Road beside the canal bridge. Retrace your steps to the station.*

5 *Turn right along a farm track at a waymark sign for the Calderdale Way. Turn left over a stone stile (waymarked) and follow a clear path across fields to a farm. Join an unmetalled road, go through the farmyard and turn right, ignoring the waymarked path.*

4 *Follow the well worn path across a field and go through a stone stile. Continue ahead keeping a wall on your left. Go through a gap on your left and follow a path ahead to some farm buildings, with the wall now on your right. Join the farm track and bear right down a steep cobbled path opposite the Top Brink Inn. Turn right along a tarmac road.*

A Nestling beside the River Calder, Todmorden has grown up at the meeting point of three valleys, incised deeply into the Pennines. For a long time the town straddled the border between Yorkshire and Lancashire, the line - marked by the infant Calder - passing under the Town Hall. However, since 1888 it has been wholly in Yorkshire. The Fielden family have always been important local benefactors and in 1875 they built the magnificent town hall. In 1782 Joshua Fielden left the family farm, purchased three cottages and started producing cotton goods. His five sons inherited the business and went on to build it into one of the largest cotton manufacturing firms in the world, with 1800 powered looms.

B The tower at Lumbutts is all that remains of Fielden's spinning mill. It once housed three water wheels arranged one above the other. They were fed by a siphon from a complex of dams behind.

Walk 18
SOWERBY BRIDGE
5 miles (8 km) Moderate

A stiff climb above the town is rewarded by fine views over the mills straggling along the Calder valley. This walk follows a fascinating series of paved paths along ways forged by a transport system from long ago. A string of charming woods lead back down into the valley and the Calder & Hebble Canal. Returning along the towpath, you will see the blockage that at present prevents a link with the Rochdale Canal and its tortuous journey across the Pennines. Attractive warehouses throng the terminal basin.

A Sowerby Bridge has been an important focus for the textile industry both as producer of cloth and manufacturer of steam engines to power the looms. Timothy Bates established the firm of Pollit & Wigzells in 1786, which went on to make huge engines of up to 1000 horse power. The overall prosperity of the town is reflected in its many fine buildings erected towards the end of the last century.

B The 253 foot (77 m) tall Wainhouse Tower, standing high above Halifax, is visible from many points on this walk.

C The attractive canal basin at Sowerby Bridge was once a hive of industry, with the large warehouses packed with goods awaiting transhipment from the Calder & Hebble to the Rochdale Canal and vice versa. The lack of a standard waterway 'gauge', usually dictated by the dimensions of the locks, led to the laborious unloading and loading of boats where the canals of two companies met. In this instance, while the Rochdale has locks 72 feet (22 m) in length, those of its neighbour are only 57.5 feet (17.5 m). More recently, road realignment has severed the once abandoned Rochdale Canal's link with the basin. However, plans are in hand to rejoin the waterway to the basin and ultimately provide a through route to Manchester.

Sowerby Bridge, the terminus of the Calder & Hebble Navigation

Over

0   1 mile

0   1 km

2 *Turn left and go ahead uphill to some railings, keeping the row of houses on your left. Bear right and follow a path to a road. Turn left and after 50 yards (45 m) turn right and climb a stile beside a waymark sign (yellow arrow). Follow a well trodden path climbing diagonally across a field to a stile.*

1 *Start from the BR station in Sowerby Bridge. There is a regular bus service (for information ring Yorkshire Rider, 0422 365985) and ample car parking space.*
Leave the station by the main exit into the car park and turn right. *Turn left up Norland Road and climb steeply to Hope Street on your left. Notice the dramatic view back over the mills of Sowerby Bridge.*

7 *Go under a railway bridge and join the canal on your left. Turn left along the towpath and walk back to Sowerby Bridge. At Albert Wood lock follow the left canal arm, passing two further locks until the canal's path is blocked by a main road beside a church. Turn left and left again down an alleyway signposted to the station. Cross the river and return to the station following the signs.*

Calder & Hebble Navigation

River Calder

A58

P   (A)

Sowerby Bridge

A58

A6026

(B)

3 *Cross the stile and continue ahead. Follow a paved path around the field boundary to the top left hand corner.* **BEWARE OF A PERMANENT ELECTRIC FENCE AROUND THIS FIELD.** *Go through a small gate, turn right and follow a wall to the top of the field. Turn left to follow a line of vertical stone slabs and go through a gate. Go ahead and through another gate to meet a tarmac road beside a pub.*

Norland Town

North Dean Wood

4 *Cross the road and go ahead following the footpath sign. Fork left at the end of a stone wall and bear diagonally downhill, aiming for a cottage roof. Notice the view over the Calder Valley towards Halifax and Wainhouse Tower. Meet a tarmac road and turn right to pass BELOW the cottages.*

5 *Follow the road through a cluster of cottages and bear left down a path signposted to North Dean Wood and Copley. Go between two parallel walls and cross a stream to continue along a paved path and through a gate. Go through another gate beside a cottage and join an unmetalled track. Maintain your direction and fork right up a signposted track (Calderdale Way).*

6 *Turn left at a waymark sign (yellow shamrock) along the top of a wood. Where two paths cross turn left to wind downhill through the wood. Meet an unmetalled track, turn right and cross the river.*

Walk 19
HEBDEN BRIDGE
4 miles (6.4km) Moderate

0   1 mile
0   1 km

A walk along a pretty, wooded stretch of the Rochdale Canal is followed by a climb up through Callis and Horsehold woods. Your efforts are rewarded by the breathtaking view over the Calder valley to the village of Heptonstall and down onto the fine old mills and cottages of Hebden Bridge.

1 Start at Hebden Bridge BR station, where you may park (charge). Hebden Bridge is 8 miles (12.8 km) north-west of Halifax on the A646. It can be reached by train from both Manchester and Leeds and is also connected by regular bus services to Halifax (for bus information ring 0422 364467).
Go down Station Road to the canal. Join the towpath and continue with the canal on your right. Just before the first lock cross the canal bridge and continue with the canal on your left. Look out for Rawden Mill Lock No.12 and cross the canal at the next bridge.

2 Leave the canal and begin the climb up the track signposted to the Pennine Way and Callis Wood. Ignore a right turn to Oaks Farm and a stile on your left. Cross a cattle grid to take a path immediately to your left through a wood, hugging the side of a hill. Descend to a makeshift gate to cross a stream on stepping stones.

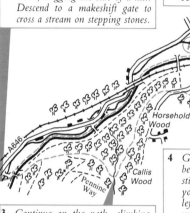

Hebden
Bridge

Rochdale Canal

A646

Horsehold
Wood

A646

Callis
Wood

Pennine
Way

3 Continue on the path, climbing into more open woodland to a seat on the summit. Continue along the path and descend to a metalled track. Turn left down the hill for 200 yards (185 m) and look for a makeshift gate on your right with a yellow waymark arrow on it.

4 Go through the gate and walk beside the top of a wall to cross a stile. Go ahead with a fence on your left. Cross a stile on your left, then turn right up an unmetalled track. Look for a waymarked stone stile on your left. Climb over and follow a steep path downhill. Turn right across a field towards a house with a wall on your left. Bear right on an unmetalled track and left along a wall below a house. Go straight ahead, then fork left down a waymarked path. Fork left at the bottom of the hill and go straight ahead under the railway. Turn left to return to the station.

A The last working boat to travel the full course of the Rochdale Canal did so in 1937. The coming of the railway in 1841 severely damaged what had once been a thriving trade in the transportation of coal, timber, stone, grain, wool and cotton. Completed in 1804, this canal was the first to cross the Pennines. It boosted trade all along its route and encouraged the building of further mills in the valley. Although disused for many years, stretches of the canal have now been restored and are fast becoming popular with boaters, walkers and naturalists.

B The woollen industry had its beginnings in the nearby village of Heptonstall, where weavers worked in their homes. The introduction of steam power brought mills to the area and so the town of Hebden Bridge developed along the valley. Rows of split-level terraced housing, provided by the mill owners for the workers, can still be seen clinging to the hillside. The upper storeys are often reached from the upper level of the hill. Many of these consisted of workers' houses with the overseer's house at the end of the row.

Walk 20
SALTERHEBBLE
3 miles (4.8 km) Easy

This route provides an excellent introduction to a surprisingly charming stretch of the Calder & Hebble Canal, together with splendid views over the Calder Valley and open countryside beyond. The canal basin at Elland offers interest and a splash of waterways colour.

1 *Start from the Jenny Dee pub, which is beside Salterhebble Basin, on the A629. A regular bus service from Halifax, Sowerby Bridge and Huddersfield stops here (for bus information ring 0422 364467), and cars can be parked nearby in Bankhouse Lane.*
Walk uphill along the A629 towards Halifax. Turn left along Bankhouse Lane and go ahead with the basin and canal on your left. Go on (ignoring a path veering right uphill) and meet a main road. Follow signs to the Calder & Hebble Canal and Salterhebble Locks.

2 *Join the towpath at Salterhebble Locks and the junction with the old Halifax Canal branch. Walk along the towpath with the canal on your left.*

3 *Continue on the towpath, passing under a skewed railway bridge, and cross the canal by a foot-bridge at the next lock. Follow the towpath through Elland Basin. Leave the canal where the towpath terminates at a flyover. Go under the flyover and follow the pavement for approximately 300 yards (275 m).*

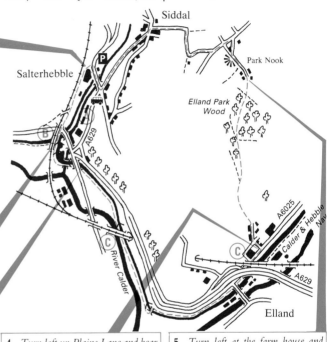

Siddal

Salterhebble

Park Nook

Elland Park Wood

River Calder

A629

A6025

Calder & Hebble Nav

A629

Elland

4 *Turn left up Plains Lane and bear right along the front of a row of stone cottages. Follow a brick paved track steadily uphill, into a wood to where three paths branch off to the right. Bear slightly right, taking the first of these paths, and continue to climb through the trees. Leave the wood and go ahead, aiming for Park Nook Farm perched on a ridge.*

5 *Turn left at the farm house and follow an unmetalled track through a farmyard and onto a tarmac road. Notice the magnificent views towards Halifax and over the Calder valley. Turn left and then fork right and follow a road down a steep hill to a junction. Turn left down Cinderhills Lane and left at the next junction. Fork right down Jubilee Road to meet the A629 opposite the Jenny Dee pub.*

A The Salterhebble Canal Basin once served Halifax via a short arm with a flight of 14 locks, using a steam pump engine to recycle water back to the top. This branch was opened in 1828 and abandoned in 1942.

B The canal junction at Salterhebble Locks provides a wealth of interesting waterway features in an attractive setting. The canal crosses the Hebble Brook on a fine aqueduct close to an unusual guillotine lock, constructed in 1932 to allow for a road widening scheme.

C The two impressive railway viaducts spanning the Calder Valley connect Halifax to Sowerby Bridge and Brighouse.

Walk 21
DIGGLE
4.5 miles (7.2 km) Easy

The delightful village of Dobcross, a path across the open moorland of Lark Hill and a walk over the top of the country's longest canal tunnel combine to make this a fascinating ramble around the ancient settlement of Diggle. The canal towpath leads you past the old mills through a peaceful tract of countryside.

A The pretty village of Dobcross was once the site of many cattle fairs. The stone cottages lining its steep streets are overlooked by the church clock, known locally as the 'Dobcross Lie', because of its temperamental nature. At the top of Nicker Brow the streets open out, giving the village an almost continental atmosphere. Here you will find the Saddleworth Bank, a pretty cottage which is, in fact, the village's own private bank. During the 18th century The Swan Inn was kept by a branch of the Wrigley family, who later emigrated to America and founded the famous chewing gum empire.

The Saddleworth Bank, Dobcross

B Harrop Edge is known locally as Lark Hill. It was once common land.

C Boat Lane got its name from the days when horse-drawn boats were using the canal. As there was no towpath through the tunnel, the horse had to be walked over the top of the hill while the boatmen 'legged' the boat through, lying on their backs and walking it along against the tunnel side.

D The spoil which was excavated in order to build The Standedge Tunnel (see Walk **22**) is all around. Note the tunnel ventilation shaft behind the spoil heap.

E The three-storeyed weavers cottages in Diglea are typical of the area. Their curious design dates back to the expansion of the broadcloth weaving industry in the late 18th century. Houses had an extra storey added in order to accommodate more looms, hence the long row of windows on the upper storey, which provided more light.

F Standedge has no less than four tunnels, one for the canal and three for the railway, all exceeding 3 miles (4.8 km) in length. Today, only one railway tunnel is in use. The canal tunnel has been closed to traffic since 1944.

G Construction of the Huddersfield Narrow Canal started in 1794, and took 17 years to complete. It was officially closed in 1944. The Huddersfield Canal Society has been actively campaigning for the full restoration of the waterway, and is already well on its way towards achieving this goal.

H Shaws Pallet Works, built in 1861, was once the Dobcross Loom Works.

Over

3 *Where a concrete railing ends at Carr House, go right, down-hill. Go through a gate to your left, then over a stile. Go ahead through a garden. Ignore a track to the left at the end of the drive. Go through a gate on your left and follow a wall on your left to the road. Cross it, then join a public footpath. Aim for the top left corner of the field and squeeze through a gap in the wall. Turn left onto a track and right after a house on your right. Follow a wall to some houses. Turn left along a track, then left again where the track bears right.*

4 *Go straight ahead to climb a gate, then turn right to a stile. Bear left round a spoil heap and cross a stile on your right. Go ahead to a small gate in a wall. Cross a stile. Turn left, then right, in front of a row of garages. Go ahead through a gate to some farm buildings, then through two gates to your right to join a track. Turn right, then right again at a track junction. Continue through the cottages to cross a railway bridge.*

2 *Fork left by a chapel and go ahead until the track bears left. Cross a stile ahead and follow a path along a hill. Where the path forks, bear right and continue to a signpost to Diggle. Turn right, then immediately left and descend to a house. Go down some steps and leave by the drive to turn left at the road.*

A670

Carr

Diggle Edge

C

D

E

F Diglea

B Harrop Edge

Diggle

5 *Bear left and go through a car park to join the canal. Notice the entrance to the tunnel. Follow the towpath to Shaws Works and cross a bridge to walk with the canal on your right. Continue to the A670 and return to the car park.*

H

G

Huddersfield Narrow Canal

Dobcross

A

P

A640

A670

1 *Start from Wool Road car park, situated where the A670 crosses the Huddersfield Narrow Canal 0.5 mile (0.8 km) north of Uppermill. Bus no 233 runs here from Manchester (for information ring Busline, 061-228 7811). Turn left along the canal to the Brownhills Visitor Centre. Briefly join the main A670 road by turning left in front of the Visitor Centre. Turn left along the A640 signposted to Dobcross and after 0.25 mile (0.4 km) turn right up Brookdale, towards a church. Join a lane in front of a row of cottages. Turn right to continue to The Swan Inn, then right into Sandy Lane.*

Walk 22

THE STANDEDGE TUNNEL

0   1 mile

0   1 km

3.5 miles (5.6 km) Strenuous – parts slippery in freezing conditions

After a gentle walk down a flight of locks a steep climb takes you high above the Colne valley and the town of Marsden for a fine overview of the Huddersfield Narrow Canal, which can be seen threading its way alongside the railway. It disappears into Standedge Tunnel, the longest and highest canal tunnel in the world.

2 *Turn left up a track to a road. Turn left and immediately right under a bridge to begin a steep climb. When woodland on your left ends, turn left at a waymark sign (a green circle with a yellow arrow showing two walkers) and follow a path with a wall on your left. Cross the stream to bear left at a waymark sign. Go ahead to a track by a house and bear left at a waymark arrow.*

3 *Cross a stile beside a gate and descend to meet a track. Turn right at a waymark sign. Where two tracks cross, turn right to go uphill. Ignore a stile on your right. Go straight ahead with a house on your left. Where a track bears left go straight ahead onto open moorland. Go through a small gate beside a larger one and continue uphill.*

4 *Just beyond a disused quarry on your right turn left downhill between two walls. Continue downhill until you meet an unmetalled track. Turn right. Just before you come to a house, turn left between two stone posts, and follow the path to a signpost pointing to Tunnel End. After visiting the Information Centre, cross the canal bridge and walk back to the station with the canal on your left.*

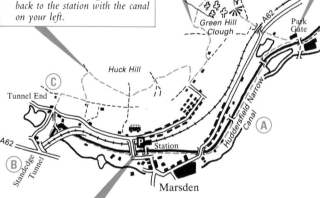

B One of the wonders of the waterways, Standedge Tunnel is 5698 yards (5210 m) long and 645 feet (197 m) above sea level, with sections lying more than 600 feet (180 m) below the surface. It carries the canal through rough blasted gritstone to emerge in Lancashire on its way to the Ashton Canal. Excavation of the tunnel was fraught with difficulties and took nearly 16 years to complete. There are four passing points in the tunnel, each of them a large cavern hewn out of the rock. Absence of a towpath meant that boats had to be 'legged' through the tunnel by men pushing against the sides of the tunnel whilst lying on their backs. This could take up to four hours with a fully laden boat. The canal tunnel has been closed to traffic since 1944.

C The cottages at Tunnel End were built originally to house tunnel keepers, whose job it was to enforce the by-laws which regulated the flow of tunnel traffic.

1 *Start from Marsden BR station on the Manchester to Huddersfield line. There is a regular bus service from Huddersfield, nos 352, 350 & 351 (for information ring Yorkshire Rider, 0484 426313). You may park at the station. Marsden is on the A62 between Manchester and Huddersfield.*

Turn right immediately outside the station to join the canal towpath. Turn right again under a bridge to walk with the canal on your left. Follow a flight of locks downhill to the edge of a reservoir. Cross a bridge, climb a ladder stile on your right and continue to the end of the reservoir.

A The Huddersfield Narrow Canal was built between 1794 and 1811 to connect the Lancashire textile towns and Huddersfield.

Walk 23

UPPERMILL

3 miles (4.8 km) Moderate

The wonderful panoramic views from the hills above Uppermill make this a worthwhile climb. The towns and villages which evolved during the industrial revolution can be seen nestling in the valleys, dominated by the spectacular scenery of Marsden Moor and the Peak District National Park.

3 Go under the railway, and turn right at the lane. Go under the railway again and look for some steps on your right. Ascend the steps onto the embankment, turn right and go ahead along the course of the railway to meet a road. Turn left and follow a sign to the Visitor Centre. Cross the canal under a viaduct and turn right along the towpath. Continue to the main road. Turn left to visit the museum.

2 Go ahead, keeping a wall on your left to climb a stile. Continue on a track, then descend with the wall still on your left to go through a stile. Bear right downhill across a golf course to a pond. BEWARE OF FLYING GOLF BALLS. Follow a yellow arrow waymark behind the pond downhill, with a wire fence on your left. Go ahead through a squeeze stile. Ignore a wooden stile on your left and descend towards a house. Follow a waymarked sign steeply downhill to a disused railway.

4 Cross the road and go down some steps to rejoin the canal. Continue to the next road bridge. Climb the steps and turn right to follow a road uphill. Ignore the first right turn, then follow the road as it bends sharp right to return to the station.

1 Start at Greenfield BR station, which is on the A670 about 4 miles (6.4km) east of Oldham. Bus no 180 runs here from Manchester (for information ring Busline, 061-228 7811). There is a car park at the station.
Turn left out of the station, then left onto a main road. Where Oaklands Road forks left, turn right up a public footpath by a lodge. Continue along the side of a hill to climb a stile. Go ahead on a wide track to where five paths cross.

A This old branch railway was opened in 1851 and was nicknamed the Delph Donkey, as the first trains which ran along the valley to nearby Delph were thought to be horse drawn. It closed in 1955.

B This wonderful railway viaduct was completed in the 1840's. Notice the skewed arch which spans the canal.

C The Saddleworth Museum was once a woollen mill. The exhibits include a full-sized model of a 19th-century clothier's cottage. A narrowboat operates trips from here during the summer, making the journey along the canal through the locks to the viaduct.

D The ultimate completion of the 20-mile (32-km) long Huddersfield Narrow Canal in 1794 enabled the transportation of raw materials and produce between Huddersfield and Manchester. The growth of the railways brought about its decline until, in 1944, the canal was finally closed to navigation and abandoned. Thirty years of dereliction rendered it unsightly and dangerous. However, in 1974 a group of enthusiasts formed the Huddersfield Canal Society, dedicated to restoring the canal to a navigable waterway. This section of the walk makes apparent some of the obstacles which they face in achieving their goal.

Walk 24

HIGH LANE

4.5 miles (7.2 km) Moderate

0 ⊢————————————————————⊣ 1 mile

0 ⊢————————————————————⊣ 1 km

The busy A6 road is soon left behind as this walk initially explores surprisingly remote farmland amongst gentle hills. The return route is via a fine stretch of rural canal, punctuated by a flurry of colourful boats moored around a boatyard on the old canal arm at Higher Poynton.

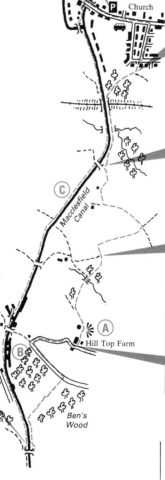

1 *Start in High Lane, a village on the A6, not far from Stockport. There is a car park across the road from The Dog & Partridge pub, and bus nos 198 & 199 between Stockport & Buxton and 361 between Stockport & Glosssop stop here (for information ring Cheshire Bus, 0625 534850). Walk along the main road with The Dog & Partridge on your right to pass the church on your left. Turn right along Brookside Lane. Take the lane to the right of the Cheshire County Stores.*

6 *Cross the foot-bridge and walk with the canal on your right. Rejoin the A6 road at steps at The Bull's Head pub. Turn right to return to the start.*

2 *At the entrance to the tennis courts, go down the path to the right. Follow this path into trees to reach the canal at a stile. Cross the stile and walk with the canal on your right.*

3 *At the next bridge, follow the track away from the canal. When you reach a T-junction, turn left over a stile beside a gate, and walk to the next gate. Turn right over a stile beside the gate and walk with a fence on your right to a stile. Cross it and turn sharp left.*

4 *Cross the next stile and walk to a gap in the trees, where there is a foot-bridge. Cross it. Veer left to a stile in the fence opposite and climb over. Walk uphill to iron railings at Hill Top Farm. Cross a stile, turn right through a gate and walk to the right of farm buildings to emerge at a road.*

5 *Turn right and follow the road when it turns sharp left. Cross a cattle grid and immediately turn right to walk with a fence on your right to a waymarked stile. Cross it and now walk with the fence on your left. When the fence turns sharp left, continue ahead to the canal. Cross an old gate and walk with the canal on your right.*

A A splendid view from Hill Top Farm towards Whaley Moor and The High Peaks.

B Subsidence from an old coal mine has caused the canal to form shallow lagoons here. Bridges and banks were once continually having to be raised to maintain the level.

C Sections of canal between locks are known as 'pounds'. At over 500 feet (152 m) above sea level, this is the highest pound in the country still open to through navigation.

BOLLINGTON VIADUCT

4 miles (6.4 km) Easy

0   1 mile

0   1 km

The handsome mill town of Bollington is situated on the edge of the Peak District. This walk takes you high above the town on both the impressive railway viaduct and the more demure canal aqueduct, where the views are at their best. Grand mill buildings, once noisy with machinery, now stand quiet.

2 *Just before the second bridge, ignore a wooden path to your right, but walk up steps to your left to join a road. Turn right. At the canal bridge, go down steps to join the towpath. Walk with the canal on your left.*

1 *Those arriving by car will find Bollington on the B5090, which is signposted to the right off the A523 coming from Macclesfield. Park in the Adlington Road Car Park & Picnic Area, which is signposted to the left just beyond the viaduct. There is a bus stop for routes 10 & 11 from Macclesfield, just below the viaduct (for information ring Cheshire Bus, 0625 534850).*
Start by taking the path by the playpark, at the rear of the car park. Walk up steps and continue ahead, away from the viaduct.

4 *Immediately after the second bridge the path diverts around an industrial estate, crosses a road and rejoins the original route. After crossing Bollington Viaduct, descend the steps to the right to return to the car park.*

3 *At bridge 29 the towpath changes sides. Cross the canal at the next bridge (no 30) and follow the path to join the Middlewood Way, a tarmac path. Turn right and continue ahead.*

A The imposing frontage of Clarence Mill towers above the canal. It was built in the 1820s by Swindell's, and was the first mill in

the town to focus on water transport. Canal boats delivered coal and raw cotton, and transported fine quality table linen and lace away. Two great steam engines, 'Perseverance' and 'Success', powered the machinery. After falling into disuse in the 1960s, the building has been restored and now houses small industrial units

B Adelphi Mill was built by Swindell's in the 1850s, for the owner's two sons. Initially dependent upon the canal, it turned its back on water transport in 1869 when the railway was built right outside its back door. Cotton silk was produced here, to be replaced after World War II by rayon and nylon seat belt webbing. Closed in the 1970s, it is now used as offices, workshops and a pub.

C This is a handsome type of change-over bridge, where the towpath switches from one side of the canal to the other. Known locally as a snake bridge, its design meant that the towing horse need not be unhitched from the boat when crossing.

D The Macclesfield, Bollington & Marple Railway opened in 1869. Now disused, it has been transformed into the Middlewood Way, used by walkers, cyclists and horse-riders. The view from the viaduct is splendid.

Walk 26
PORTLAND BASIN
3.5 miles (5.6 km) Easy

This is an attractive one way walk along canal towpaths, with the return by train (no Sunday service). It follows a route often close to the River Tame, through an area once humming with industrial activity. Today much of this area has been attractively landscaped and nature is returning. A visit to the museum at Portland Basin brings the past vividly back to life.

> **2** Turn right and walk to a canal junction. Cross both canals by the foot-bridges and visit The Portland Basin Heritage Centre. Retrace your steps across both bridges to turn left along the Peak Forest Canal and over an aqueduct.

> **1** Start from Guide Bridge BR station, which is on the A6017 Ashton-under-Lyne to Stockport road. Bus number 219 from Manchester stops here (for information ring Busline, 061-228 7811). There is car parking beside the station.
> Turn right out of the station and go across a road junction aiming for the car park to the left of the Boundary pub. Join the canal towpath by the steps behind the pub.

A The main line of the Ashton Canal, authorised in 1792 and opened soon afterwards, is only 6.5 miles (10.5 km) long and was built both to link Manchester to the coalfields around Oldham and the textile mills of Ashton. By 1962 the canal lay completely derelict and would have remained so but for the intervention of the

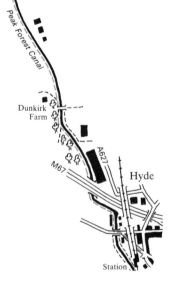

Peak Forest Canal Society and the Waterways Recovery Group. First formed in 1970, these volunteer navvies have mounted extensive campaigns – or digs – on derelict canals throughout the country and have become the backbone of a far-reaching waterways restoration movement. In 1972 more than 800 navvies, old and young, descended upon the navigation in an organised working party, providing the impetus for a grand reopening two years later.

B The Portland Basin Heritage Centre is housed in part of a warehouse built by the Ashton canal company in 1834. It was all but destroyed by fire in 1972 and rebuilt as part of a project to redevelop the Portland Basin area. The

> **3** Walk for 2 miles (3.2 km) along the towpath with the canal on your left to meet a motorway bridge. At the next bridge cross the canal, join a road, and turn right. Turn right again and come to Hyde Central BR station on your right. There is an hourly service to Guide Bridge. Check train times before starting out by by telephoning 061-832 8353. There is no Sunday service.

museum sets out the story of Tameside's social and industrial history by drawing together a series of themes, ranging from cotton spinning to Chartism and uses seven separate displays to unfold the picture. It is open daily, except Mondays, throughout the year. Times vary and can be checked by telephoning 061-308 3374. Free.

Walk 27

WOODLEY TUNNEL

3.5 miles (5.6 km) Easy

0   1 mile

0   1 km

The Peak Forest Canal is at its prettiest as it leads the walker through a tree-lined avenue to the River Tame, keeping industry at a distance. The return beside the flowing water of the river provides a contrast with the still canal. A rare chance to walk through a canal tunnel adds a little excitement.

3 Walk along the river bank to meet some steps and follow a sign to Meadow Lane, keeping along the bank. Turn right and follow a sign to Stockport Road. After 100 yards (90 m) turn left in front of a white house to follow a sign to Stockport Road and Hulmes Wood.

4 Turn left across the river, following signs to Marple, and then left to follow a sign to Woodley. Fork right up an unmetalled track ignoring a sign to the canal. Pass Botany Mill and maintain your direction through a housing estate to turn right at a T-junction. Turn left along Mill Lane, cross a railway, and go ahead along Mill Street.

5 Turn right along Hyde Road and left at some traffic lights up George Lane. Where the road bends right turn left along Gilbert Bank and go downhill to the canal. Descend the steps on the right to join the towpath and turn left. Go through Woodley Tunnel, under a skew bridge and meet the bridge where you first joined the canal. Retrace your steps to the station.

2 Walk for approximately 1 mile (1.6 km) and look for a signpost to the River Tame 150 yards (135 m) before a metal foot-bridge over the canal. Turn left and follow a cobbled path down to the river. Cross the river and turn left to follow the sign to Haughton Dale.

1 Start from the BR station at Woodley, which lies on the A560 midway between Stockport and Ashton-under-Lyne. Bus numbers 192 and 193 run from Manchester to Stockport and number 330 from Stockport to Woodley (for information ring Busline, 061-228 7811). There is car parking at the station.
Turn left out of the station, then right, and immediately left to go downhill. When the road bears left go ahead down a cobbled path and join the canal. Go over a bridge and turn right along the towpath.

A The Peak Forest Canal owes its origins to the great deposits of limestone at Doveholes, near Whaley Bridge (see Walk 29). Like its neighbour, the Ashton Canal, it was derelict in the 1960s, and was finally restored for navigation in 1974.

B The remaining gardens and grounds of Apethorn House are well worth visiting. Turn left through a gateway at the bottom of the cobbled path and follow an anti-clockwise circuit. William Sidebotham, with the help of a fortune made in the Cheshire salt industry (see Walk **15**), built an impressive house here in 1760, close to the cotton mills that he had established nearby. Only the remains of an extensive garden are left, including a range of shrubs and trees not native to this country and thought to be gifts from buyers and friends abroad. The house and original mills on the site of the Gee Cross Mill (across the canal and now demolished) were later purchased by the Ashton family. In 1831 the eldest son, Thomas, was murdered in nearby Apethorn Lane, by a man that he had discharged on the previous day, for being a member of a trade union.

C Woodley Tunnel is 176 yards (161 m) long. It is unusual in being a narrow tunnel with the towpath continuing through it.

43

MARPLE JUNCTION

6 miles (9.7 km) Moderate

A charming length of the Peak Forest Canal leads the walker across a splendid stone aqueduct over the River Goyt, to join ancient woodlands above the historic settlement of Chadkirk. Re-crossing the Goyt, the return is by way of open countryside and the impressive Marple lock flight.

A Marple Aqueduct was completed in 1800 and carries the Lower Peak Forest Canal 97 feet (30 m) over the River Goyt. Its designer, Benjamin Outram, copied the ideas of William Edwards by piercing the shoulders of each arch. These holes are both decorative and functional, reducing the weight of the rubble filling which would otherwise bear directly on each pier. Two different colours of gritstone were used in the construction of the parapets and ledges to add contrast and interest.

B Chadkirk Country Park is unusual in that it is centred on a 59 acre (24 hectare) working farm, run at a profit. Visitors can follow an excellent trail and glean all relevant information from the well laid out interpretation boards. Several picnic areas are also provided. There is also a 14th-century chapel on the site of a monastic cell founded by St. Chad, which is now the Visitor Centre.

C Opened in 1831 and surveyed by Thomas Telford, the Macclesfield Canal was one of the last canals to be built. Some of its promoters even saw it as a possible route for a railway (to replace the canal if that should become uneconomic) and it was consequently made quite shallow. In common with all Telford's designs it was of a 'cut and fill' construction, following as straight a course as possible. Its main traffic was coal, and cotton from the large mills beside its northern reaches.

D Whilst the Peak Forest Canal was opened in 1800 the impressive flight of locks at Marple was not completed until four years later, when the canal company had raised the necessary £27,000. In the meantime, cargo was transhipped onto a temporary tramway system, using iron box containers with a two ton payload. The locks raise the canal 214 feet (65 m) within a distance of 1 mile (1.6 km).

Marple Junction.

Over

MARPLE JUNCTION
Continued

0   1 mile

0   1 km

3 Turn left and follow the lane to Otterspool Road. Turn left and cross a river into Dooley Lane to go ahead up a hill to a junction. Turn right, then left at some traffic lights up Offerton Road. Turn left at Yew Tree Farm Nursery and go across the yard to a stile.

1 Start from Marple BR station, which is also served by regular buses from Manchester via Stockport (for information ring Busline, 061-228 7811). There is ample car parking at the station. Turn right up Brabyns Brow and meet the canal. Turn right and walk along the towpath for 1.25 miles (2 km).

2 Follow a path over Hydebank Tunnel, join an unmetalled track and bear left by Hyde Farm. Fork left at a sign to Valley Way (waymarked with a white footprint) to briefly rejoin the canal. Fork left at a sign to Valley Way and Chadkirk and follow the wide, well walked path through woods, and down steps, to meet a lane.

5 Turn left to follow a waymark sign (blue man) across a golf course soon after the estate ends. Beware of flying golf balls. Ignore the waymark sign through the estate (yellow arrow). Go ahead along the boundary of the golf course, look for a gap in a hedge, and meet a copse beside a stream. Follow the waymark signs (blue man and yellow arrow) to rejoin the golf course.

4 Cross the stile and follow a track uphill, signed to Marple. Maintain your direction along the top of a copse aiming diagonally across a field towards a prominent signpost in the corner. Turn left and cross a stile following the sign to Buxton Lane. Follow a path through a wood and across a stream to meet a farm track. Go ahead, following a waymark sign (yellow arrow), cross a cattle grid, and turn right just before a housing estate along the waymarked Holly Trail.

6 Keeping the stream on your left, follow the waymark signs (blue man), maintaining your direction across the golf course, aiming to the right of a large mill. When you come to the canal, turn left along the towpath, and walk to a canal junction.

7 Cross the canal and bear left down a flight of locks. Follow the towpath to bridge 17 and turn right down Brabyns Brow retracing your steps to the station.

Peak Forest Canal

Aqueduct

Station

River Goyt

A626

Yewtree Farm

Marple Junction

Marple

Macclesfield Canal

Golf course

Walk 29

NEW MILLS, BUXWORTH & WHALEY BRIDGE

8 miles (12.9 km) Moderate

There is an enormous variety of architectural interest along this route, as well as calm waterside walking and fine views. The valley of the River Goyt had for years been an ancient drovers route and, today, three means of transport – road, rail and water – are crammed in between the hills. The river was at one time a source of water power, allowing industry to establish itself here at the beginning of the industrial revolution. When coal mining began in the valley, there was an explosion of manufacturing. In today's terms, however, it was all at a very small scale, and sufficiently scattered that it did not dominate the landscape – an enclosed river valley well endowed with trees. The industrial archaeology of the canal basins at Buxworth and Whaley Bridge is both picturesque and fascinating and, surprisingly, there is peace and quiet in the midst of all this activity. This route can be linked with Walk **30**, as they both start from the same place.

A The stone buildings at Goytside Farm form an attractive group around a paved and cobbled yard. The earliest record of a farm here dates from 1627, although it was almost certainly farmed prior to that.

B The intricate basins at Buxworth were originally the terminus of the Peak Forest Canal, with the line to Whaley Bridge being a branch. Today it is Buxworth which has the lesser status of a branch. In their heyday in the 1880s, when Buxworth was called Bugsworth, over 600 tons of limestone and lime was loaded into 30 or 40 narrowboats each day, having been brought from the great quarries at Doveholes, some 6.5 miles (10.5 km) away. Buxworth was connected to these quarries by the Peak Forest Tramway, built in 1799. Until its demise in 1926, the wagons on this plate tramway were exclusively horse drawn, apart from a 500 yard (460 m) inclined plane at Chapel-en-le-Frith. Here, loaded wagons pulled empty ones up a 1 in 7.5 slope by means of a continuous rope.

Having lain disused since 1926, the basins became silted and overgrown. Restoration work by the Inland Waterways Preservation Society and British Waterways will eventually see them open and in water, and the Navigation Inn will once again overlook a busy waterways scene.

C On this walk, the approach to the canal basin at Whaley Bridge is made down a straight path, following the course of what was once an inclined plane. This was part of the 33-mile (53 km) long Cromford & High Peak Railway, which connected the Peak Forest Canal with the Cromford Canal, which, in turn, joined the River Trent. It was part of a grand scheme, never brought to completion, to construct a canal/rail line from London to Manchester via Leicester.

Built to the standard gauge, this remarkable railway reached a height of 1200 feet (366 m) above sea level, and had numerous steep slopes and inclined planes where steam engines, some locomotive, some stationary, heaved wagons up slopes as steep as 1 in 7. Sec-

tions of the line stayed in use until 1967, but now large parts have been turned into footpaths and bridleways.

D Bank End Bridge, number 29, stands unaltered since it was built in the late 18th century. A grade II listed building, its stones are cut with grooves made by the towing ropes of countless horse drawn narrowboats.

E This splendid 13 arch sandstone railway viaduct strides purposefully across the flood plain of the River Goyt. It was built in 1902 by the Midland Railway Company to provide a more direct route to Manchester Central station. For many years it was used only by goods trains carrying limestone from Buxton to the chemical works around Northwich, but in 1986 a link was opened at Hazel Grove, providing a through route for main line trains from Liverpool and Manchester to Sheffield – traffic more worthy of its grand scale.

Over

NEW MILLS, BUXWORTH
Continued **& WHALEY BRIDGE**

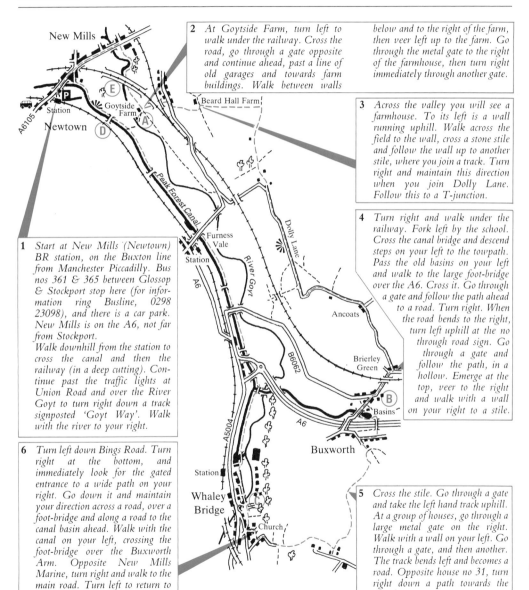

2 *At Goytside Farm, turn left to walk under the railway. Cross the road, go through a gate opposite and continue ahead, past a line of old garages and towards farm buildings. Walk between walls below and to the right of the farm, then veer left up to the farm. Go through the metal gate to the right of the farmhouse, then turn right immediately through another gate.*

3 *Across the valley you will see a farmhouse. To its left is a wall running uphill. Walk across the field to the wall, cross a stone stile and follow the wall up to another stile, where you join a track. Turn right and maintain this direction when you join Dolly Lane. Follow this to a T-junction.*

4 *Turn right and walk under the railway. Fork left by the school. Cross the canal bridge and descend steps on your left to the towpath. Pass the old basins on your left and walk to the large foot-bridge over the A6. Cross it. Go through a gate and follow the path ahead to a road. Turn right. When the road bends to the right, turn left uphill at the no through road sign. Go through a gate and follow the path, in a hollow. Emerge at the top, veer to the right and walk with a wall on your right to a stile.*

1 *Start at New Mills (Newtown) BR station, on the Buxton line from Manchester Piccadilly. Bus nos 361 & 365 between Glossop & Stockport stop here (for information ring Busline, 0298 23098), and there is a car park. New Mills is on the A6, not far from Stockport.*
Walk downhill from the station to cross the canal and then the railway (in a deep cutting). Continue past the traffic lights at Union Road and over the River Goyt to turn right down a track signposted 'Goyt Way'. Walk with the river to your right.

6 *Turn left down Bings Road. Turn right at the bottom, and immediately look for the gated entrance to a wide path on your right. Go down it and maintain your direction across a road, over a foot-bridge and along a road to the canal basin ahead. Walk with the canal on your left, crossing the foot-bridge over the Buxworth Arm. Opposite New Mills Marine, turn right and walk to the main road. Turn left to return to the start.*

5 *Cross the stile. Go through a gate and take the left hand track uphill. At a group of houses, go through a large metal gate on the right. Walk with a wall on your left. Go through a gate, and then another. The track bends left and becomes a road. Opposite house no 31, turn right down a path towards the church.*

THE GOYT VALLEY

5 miles (8 km) Easy – apart from a short rough path through trees

An outward journey beside the swiftly flowing River Goyt contrasts well with the tranquil canalside return on this walk.

There is always plenty of interest – small scale mills built during the industrial revolution nestle above the weirs in the gorge, while trains, deep in tree lined cuttings, whiz in and out of Disley Tunnel. This route can be linked with Walk 29, as they both start from the same place.

4 *Pass through a rough squeeze stile above a weir. After 15 yards (14 m) veer diagonally left up through trees to shortly join a lane by houses. Turn right. Join a main road and turn left.*

3 *At the 30 mph sign, take the path to the right, which soon doubles back up the hill to join another path. Turn right. This path joins a road, where you turn right. Walk past the entrance barrier at the paper mill and follow the lane up through the back of the works to rejoin the river on your right. Continue.*

2 *Turn left between houses, following 'The Goyt Way' sign. Cross a stile by a metal gate and continue with the river to your left, over a stile and through three kissing gates to join a road. Turn left and walk over the bridge.*

5 *By the name sign for Strines village, turn left up a wide track. Continue through a gateway to reach the canal at Strines Aqueduct. Walk up the bank to your left to walk with the canal on your right. Just beyond bridge 28 and opposite New Mills Marine, turn left along Victoria Street to join the main road. Turn left to return to the start.*

1 *Start at New Mills (Newtown) BR station, on the Buxton line from Manchester Piccadilly. Bus nos 361 & 365 between Glossop & Stockport stop here (for information ring Busline, 0298 23098), and there is a car park. New Mills is on the A6, not far from Stockport.*

Walk downhill from the station, cross the canal and turn left along Wirksmoor Road. Walk ahead following signs for 'The Goyt Way'. At a factory entrance descend steps on your left, cross a foot-bridge and turn left. Walk past a gate to join a road. Continue ahead.

A Torr Vale Mill is the last remaining working mill in New Mills, now producing cotton towelling products. Built in 1788, it was originally powered by a water wheel, which was augmented by a steam engine in 1856. Electricity was installed in 1931. Water power was abandoned and the steam engine was removed in 1951. The present occupants, W. S. Lowe, have been here since 1864.

B The River Goyt, together with the River Sett which joins it in New Mills, formed this steep gorge during the ice age, cutting through soft sandstone. Building weirs enabled a good head of water to be obtained to turn the waterwheels needed to power new spinning machines, invented by pioneers such as Arkwright, some two centuries ago.

C Opposite the old canal wharf is Hawthorns' Canal Foundry, which traded for 90 years until closure in 1989.